Hayloft to Liftoff

A Biography of Leister F. Graffis

by

Ethel M. Rutt

DORRANCE PUBLISHING CO., INC.
PITTSBURGH, PENNSYLVANIA 15222

ISBN # 0-8059-3970-9
Printed in the United States of America

Second Printing

For information or to order additional books, please write:
Dorrance Publishing Co., Inc.
643 Smithfield Street
Pittsburgh, Pennsylvania 15222
U.S.A.
1-800-788-7654

*The life of Leister F. Graffis was told to
Ethel M. Rutt by friends, Leister himself,
and his wife, Marian Ammann Graffis.*

Dedication

*To my parents, Runnion and May Graffis,
whose example and guidance laid the
foundation for my life of miracles*

Contents

Acknowledgments

Hayloft to Liftoff was made possible by the understanding and patience of my husband and my treasured friends, Virginia and William Maxim who did the initial proofreading and typing of the story.

This biography resorts repeatedly to quotations from the King James Version of the Bible to affirm the mutual faith and philosophy of Marian and Leister Graffis.

Foreword

The biography of Leister F. Graffis is a story of the triumph of faith.

Dr. Henry B. Wilson of Baltimore, Maryland, diagnosed a structural congenital defect in the center of the retinas of both of Leister's eyes which caused loss of visual acuity and altered perception or interpretation. The defect was so unique that Dr. Wilson referred Leister to the Wilmer Eye Clinic of Johns Hopkins University. They were so impressed with the anomaly, they requested to make a longitudinal study of his eyes.

A handicap of this dimension would have caused many to resign themselves to dependency. Leister never permitted his handicap to sideline him and with undaunted faith in the power of his Sovereign Lord, he believed that he could perfect his strength in this very weakness. His faith was honored and blindness of sight was seemingly given a double portion of acuity in perception and perseverance so not only did he keep pace, but he far surpassed multitudes who did not labor under handicap.

His story is written as told to me. By extensive research the first chapter seeks to portray the mood of the times in which Leister was born. Simple anecdotes in Chapter One are probabilities based on the personality of the times in which Leister was born.

Marian Ammann is introduced in Chapter Nine. I shift the story to first person at that point and with her permission write the balance of Leister's story as she alone could know it.

Ethel M. Rutt
Willow Valley Manor

Chapter One
Reaching for the Moon

There had been a touch of frost on the pumpkins. The corn had turned brown, and the trees were staging a brilliant autumn color parade. Runnion Graffis drove the horses slowly down the rows to gather in the corn he had husked that afternoon after school. These were busy days. He loaded more pumpkins to store with the late apples. There yet remained carrots, beets, and celery to glean. The turnips could wait, and even the cabbages could stand a bit more frost.

With teaching school, harvesting the crops, and caring for the animals, there was little time for socialization. What complicated matters was the fact that his wife May hadn't been feeling well again. She was experiencing some of the same problems she had known less than two years ago when they learned she was to become a mother for the first time.

The prospect brought to both Runnion and May mingled emotions of fear and hope. Fear because the grass had barely covered the little grave in Green Valley Cemetery where they had buried their first child, a little daughter they had named Frances Marie. It had been so hard for Grandfather Perdue to accept that loss. Must May suffer all this again only to come through with empty arms and a broken heart?

It would be several weeks before the school board would hand him his eighty dollar check for his September salary. There were bills to pay that were made during the summer months when they had only the farm income and had farm help to pay. The money he got from the store-keeper who bought his butter and eggs was a real help. Tomorrow he would take their butter and eggs. What he got for them would be enough to pay the doctor. The grocer was glad to buy May's butter.

She had a beautiful butter mold and was so careful about her butter that the grocer welcomed it. In fact he would set it back to take home for his own use.

While May was with the doctor, Runnion was absorbed in reading an article in *Collier's* about the Wright brothers' plane. He was completely absorbed in the story of their flight and the government's interest in the project. An old retired farmer looked over his shoulder and interrupted his reading. "You reading about those Wright brothers, are you? I'd say that's robbery to spend our tax money on such fool projects."

May came out of the doctor's office flushed and smiling. After Runnion helped her into the wagon she said, "Dr. Fink thinks we are going to have another child. He said I wasn't to be afraid. He would do all he could to help us have a healthy child this time. He gave me some tonic to take which he feels certain will help me carry our child. I am sure this will be great news for my father."

The morning sickness ran its course, and the whole household was happy in anticipation. The baby clothes so tearfully tucked away were lovingly brought out and checked in readiness for their promised child, and May's heart was comforted and encouraged.

If the older folks frowned on the Wright brothers' exploits, the teacher of the Sandbur School had younger thoughts. Runnion read all he could find and sparked his pupil's imaginations. He even helped the students at recess to fold paper airplanes. Pages were brought from outdated Sears Roebuck catalogs. These old "wish books"[1] were taken to the outhouse, and children would rob them and tuck them in their schoolbags to use in flying contests. The teacher joined at recess in cheering and congratulating the ones whose planes went the farthest or highest.

In geography classes the teacher excited the children's enthusiasm with news about Robert Peary. He had them look up all they could find about the Arctic Circle, draw maps of the area, and write reports. The young and the brave were waiting in expectancy to find out if Robert Peary would succeed in his determination to plant the Stars and Stripes at the North Pole. Months had passed since he left the ship *Roosevelt* and started northward. He needed to travel four hundred miles by dogsled in weather so cold whiskey would freeze in his inside pocket.

Again the older and wiser were shaking their heads. "Why did that cowboy in the White House use tax money for such a crazy project? They deserve to get their toes frozen."

On 6 April 1901, with four Eskimos and a colored companion, Robert Peary planted the Stars and Stripes at the North Pole. Directly under the North Star, Old Glory waved three months before the world was to know, for there were no short-wave radios yet employed to keep a waiting world in touch with their travels.[2]

Peary and the Wright brothers were a reflection of the optimism and adventurous mood of the times. The robust leadership of Teddy Roosevelt for seven years had given the country a youthful mentality. The president's son, Kermit, reflected that confidence when he trustingly asked his dad, "Father, get me the moon and bring it to me?"[3]

It had been a difficult winter for May. Runnion was grateful to know as he left the house each morning to teach that her father, William Perdue, was with May. He was a faithful support to his daughter those months of expectancy. Grandfather Perdue was truly emotionally involved in the anxiety and anticipation of those months.

He became even more indispensable after 7 May 1909, when not one child, but two robust baby boys came to end the apprehension. Each of the twins weighed nearly eight pounds, and they were named Leister and Lester. A proud grandfather gave his full measure of devotion to the boys and their happy parents.

The boys came as a challenge and fulfillment to the whole household, but none of them in their fondest aspirations for the infant boys could have guessed the moon dreams Leister, the eldest of the twins, would dream; nor could they have guessed that some day he would give his support to teams that would plant the Stars and Stripes in a spot far more inaccessible than the North Pole.

Runnion Abraham Graffis 1875-1955
Nancy May Perdue 1878-1969
Married 21 August 1903

House where twins were born near Green Valley, Illinois, 7 May 1909,
with Grandpa Perdue, Runnion and May, and the twins, Lester and Leister.

Runnion's first school on Sand Prairie. Taught two years, 1901 and 1902.

Chapter Two
Green Valley Grieves

Working was a frolic for four-year-old Leister and Lester. As they pulled their little wagon full of ears of corn it was fun to throw the ears down by the chicken coop and watch the chickens and hear their cackling as they scrambled for the corn. To the twins, feeding the pigs, horses, and cows was more of a lark than real work, and they enjoyed every minute of it. They had never heard of child labor laws nor would they have been impressed had they heard.

Now that spring had come and Father was out of school, he might finish his work in time to play ball with them before Mother had supper prepared. When they had completed their chores they put their little wagon in the house, got a ball, and started passing in hopeful anticipation that Father would join them.

Finally it was time for supper. What welcome news to two hungry boys. They hurried into the house, washed their hands, and after Grandpa Perdue had checked their hands and faces, found their places at the table. Soon the whole family was gathered around the table. There never was a lack of wholesome food, for Mother was an excellent cook and gardener. She canned fruits and vegetables and made jellies in abundance. Always there were fresh eggs, homemade butter, and all kinds of meats from chicken to pork and beef raised and butchered right on their own farm.

After supper Grandpa Perdue entertained the boys with a picture book as they joined him on the wicker rocking chair. They took turns spelling out words for him, for already they knew and could write their A-B-Cs. Once in a while a naughty twin would take a wisp of their grandpa's beard and wrap it around a finger. That was when they were feeling fine. In times not so happy that white beard was a favorite haven for their troubled heads.

When the table was cleared Father turned up the lamp and spent time teaching the boys. Already they knew all the states and capitals and the names of all the presidents of the United States up to Woodrow Wilson. They had already memorized the Twenty-third Psalm and could tell the story that went with any picture in Margaret Sangster's *Bible Story Book*.

When the dishes were washed Mother was ready to join the family. May was not a seamstress or interested in any kind of knitting or needlework. She limited her activity with needles to simple mending of the family clothing and was instead an avid reader.

Everybody from Grandpa Perdue to the twins stopped everything when she took up a book and started to read aloud. May had never gone to college but was so gifted in reading that she was often asked to give readings at church and community events. Each new Sears Roebuck order would usually include one or two new books. She read such contemporary writers as Booth Tarkington and Gene Stratton Porter. She subscribed to many magazines and read all their serial stories to the family. She had a gift for interpreting poetry, and her public readings, all recited from memory, might include selections from such homespun poets as Whittier or Longfellow.

By nine o'clock Grandpa Perdue and the twins were in bed. At last May and Runnion had time to be alone. May picked up her Bible, and Runnion began to delve into the two newspapers he had selected to have delivered to the house daily. After a time Runnion dropped his paper to tell May that a farm they wished they had been able to buy had been sold for sixteen hundred dollars. They knew in their boldest fantasies they never could afford a farm at that price, nor could any other young couple at that time. Their only hope of owning a farm was if they were among the fortunate few to inherit one. This news article only confirmed their convictions that there was really no future them in Illinois on an eighty dollar a month teacher's salary.[1]

May understood it all too well. The twins were growing rapidly and planning for their future was May and Runnion's greatest concern. Only a few more weeks and with the blessing of the Lord there would be a third child. How often she and Runnion had talked over his Red River Valley dream, and always they would come to the same impasse, Grandpa Perdue. He had become such a part of the twins' lives it would be unthinkable to rob them of the comfort and security they found in his care. It would be just as unthinkable to ask Grandpa Perdue to break ties at eighty years of age and start a new life hundreds of miles from all that was home to him. Both May and Runnion knew in their hearts that memories were being stored in the minds of their sons that would grow more sacred with time. For the time it was better to dream than to act.

Weariness overtook May, and she went to bed leaving Runnion to his papers. The evening air drifting southward into Green Valley was besot with the breath of the breweries. As he read, he found a news article about the "Whiskey Trust" and the increased production of liquor that resulted from the centralization of breweries in Peoria and Pekin.[2] This only added smog to his bewilderment. What effect would this expansion of the brewery businesses all around them have on the economy and quality of life in quiet Green Valley? Was that the type of community in which he wanted to raise his children?

Forebears of the Graffis family, Nicholas and Martin Graffius, had become quite affluent by building distilleries and sending their corn to market as whiskey, but that was before the time of the railroads. Runnion rationalized that whiskey was less bulky to transport than its equivalent in corn. That had also been true in Pennsylvania and Maryland, and in days when life was simpler.[3]

He turned to the classified section. There they were again, large ads by the Great Northern and Northern Pacific Railroads offering land for sale. They called the Red River Valley Territory the "bread basket of the world," and described the region as "the land of...free homesteaders and town site boomers."[4] He clipped out an ad that looked like an answer to his dreams. It was in the *Green Valley Newspaper* and extolled the good farmland in the Red River Valley of Richland County, North Dakota.

Only a few weeks later Runnion was again reading his papers when he was interrupted abruptly by a call from May saying he should go for Dr. Fink. She was sure they would need him very soon. Runnion hurried to the barn where in anticipation of this moment he had things ready for a quick trip. That evening of 1 June 1913 was a pleasantly warm evening. Runnion drove his horse so urgently that by the time he returned to the house with Dr. Fink the horse was in a sweat. Grandpa Perdue was waiting to care for the horse while the father and doctor hastened to be with May.

Empathy for the travail May was experiencing brought beads of perspiration to the expectant father's brow. At last when he held a new son in his arms, his heart was overwhelmed again with the miracle of a new life.

The twins were told that there might be a new baby in the family in the morning when they awoke, so they were moved to Grandpa Perdue's room. They were told Mother would be busy welcoming the new baby and they were to sleep in Grandpa's room, so he could help them if they needed someone during the night.

Grandpa Perdue attended the twins very closely when they awakened in the morning. After they had breakfast Father came and took them up to their mother's room and showed them their new brother, baby Marshall. Their amazement abounded when they were told to sit and for a moment hold little baby Marshall in their arms.

A neighbor girl came to help in the home for a time. Grandpa Perdue wisely helped the twins adjust and relate to a new baby in the household. May gained strength gradually, and as the summer garden began to yield, the concerned grandfather was tireless in devotion to his daughter and grandsons. With remarkable vigor he helped harvest crops, prepare them for canning, and assist as babysitter.

In the midst of all the busy days of planting and harvesting, Runnion's mind was preoccupied with another matter. He had been asked to accept the position of principal of the Green Valley High School. This was not really what he wanted. For a long time he had wished to pack away the McGuffy readers and exchange his teaching career for a life dedicated to farm and family. Although he was rated as one of the best teachers and was receiving one of the highest salaries paid to teachers in that area, he labored under a great emotional stress in teaching.

As time passed a new concern came to the household that eclipsed all other anxieties. Grandpa Perdue complained of stomach discomfort. The old gentleman had a mind of his own and refused to consult the tried and trusted Dr. Fink. He chose to see Dr. Kelly, a doctor new to Green Valley. This doctor's medicine brought no relief, and the dear old man's condition worsened.

Finally when Dr. Kelly came to the house he declared that an operation was necessary, which he would perform on the spot. He incised the old man's abdomen without anesthesia. The old man's moans and screams became so terrifying May gathered up the children and took them to the barn until the doctor drove away.

When May returned to the house she was not prepared for what she found. As she went to her father's bedside, blood was everywhere. In the process of operating on the patient the doctor had shaken blood from his hands, and the walls, and even the ceiling were spattered with blood. The sight overwhelmed the distraught daughter.

After two agonizing weeks Grandpa Perdue was released from his pain. The whole community grieved at the passing of the beloved man. Following the funeral the undertaker said that what he found in the old man's body would support a lawsuit. Soon after the episode Dr. Kelly left Green Valley.

As he fondly packed away the personal effects of the departed, Runnion faced life from a new perspective. He pulled out the ads about North Dakota. He began to respond to those ads and said "No" to the principalship of Green Valley High School. With three children and without Grandpa Perdue's help, May would need him near. Three lively boys would help distract May's mind from the two graves in Green Valley. The haunting memory of her father's last days might best be eased in a new setting. Again Green Valley grieved when they learned their good neighbors the Graffises were going westward.

Chapter Three
A Westward Trend

As Runnion Graffis prepared to leave Green Valley, Illinois, and move to the Red River Valley of eastern North Dakota, he was in reality only extending the westward movement begun by past generations of what was in earlier days the Graffius family.

Somewhere in France in the early days of 1749 Nicholas Martin Graffius and his wife Anne Catharine pored over a pamphlet that was being circulated in Europe by the son of an admiral, Sir William Penn. It told how Charles II had borrowed large sums of money from the admiral, and in payment for the borrowed money the king had given the admiral a large tract of land in the New World. Now the admiral's son, William, was advertising the lands. He called these lands "Penn's Woods" in honor of his father. Young Penn chartered and advertised the land as a "Holy Experiment" which was to be a refuge for the victims of religious persecution.

Although Nicholas Graffius was in France, he was not French. As early as 1560, Protestants were called Huguenots in France. Older members of the Huguenot church which Nicholas attended knew of early cruel massacres of their own church people.[1] To him, religious freedom was something worth sacrificing for. When he spoke of migrating, the elders in the church encouraged Nicholas and Anne. In reality many other young people were hearing the westward call.

Nicholas was actually a German citizen and there was a rumor that he used the money he had intended to purchase immunity from German military service to purchase his passage to America. On 15 September 1749, Nicholas, Anne Catherine, a three-year-old son Nicholas, and five-month-old son Peter boarded a ship called the *Edinburg* at Rotterdam and sailed for the New World. They went first to Germantown but finally settled in York County, Pennsylvania, where eight more children were born. This continued a westward trend that succeeding generations were to extend to the western coast of the United States.

In revolutionary days the American Congress met in the York County Court House, bringing the hub of colonial activity into the area where Nicholas Graffius had settled. By then the three-year-old immigrant Nicholas Graffius was an adult and served as a sharpshooter under General Daniel Morgan. This also was to be the beginning of a family tradition. The son of Nicholas Martin Graffius served in the War of 1812, and a grandson, Abraham Graffius, served in the Civil War. It was for Leister Graffis to follow this tradition and rise to serve as a lieutenant commander in World War II.

President of the United States of America.

To all who shall see these presents, greeting:

Know Ye, that reposing special Trust and Confidence in the Patriotism, Valor, Fidelity and Abilities of _____LEISTER FINK GRAFFIS_____ I do appoint him

_____A LIEUTENANT COMMANDER_____

in the Naval Reserve of The United States Navy to rank from the _____ ---- _____ day of _____ ---- _____ He is therefore carefully and diligently to discharge the duties of such office by doing and performing all manner of things thereunto belonging.

And I do strictly charge and require all Officers, Seamen and Marines under his Command to be obedient to his orders. And he is to observe and follow such orders and directions from time to time, as he shall receive from me, or the future President of The United States of America, or his Superior Officer set over him, according to the Rules and Discipline of the Navy.

This Commission to continue in force during the pleasure of the President of the United States, for the time being.

Done at the City of Washington, this _____SECOND_____ day of _____MAY_____ in the year of our Lord One Thousand Nine Hundred and _____FORTY-NINE_____ and of the Independence of The United States of America, the One Hundred and

SEVENTY-THIRD.

By the President:

John L. Sullivan
Secretary of the Navy

428789

Relative Precedence from 1 January 1946

Abraham's father, Jacob, had taken a step in the westward movement and moved his family to Indiana. This western branch of the Graffius family dropped the "u" from the name of Graffius and became the Graffis line of the family.

Leister's grandfather, Abraham Graffis, married his cousin, Sarah Elizabeth Enyeart. In later years this inter-family marriage was speculated as a possible etiology for the congenital eye weakness of the twin boys Leister and Lester Graffis. His cousin Sarah bore Abraham thirteen children, two of which died early in life. When Abraham Graffis died at the age of fifty-three, his forty-three-year-old wife Sarah took another step westward and moved her family to Natrona, Illinois. This widowed mother was unable to read or write and supported her children by hard manual labor.

Leister's father Runnion Graffis was eleven years old when his father died, so he learned the meaning of the work ethic, "He who does not work, does not eat." As soon as they were able, the children did whatever they could to support the family. Runnion attended the local school and then studied at the Illinois State Normal School. He was an avid sportsman and counted the day when he helped his football team take the championship from Northwestern a red letter day in his career. After Normal School he taught school for twelve years in Tazell County, Illinois.

Runnion's older brother, Levi, had become a streetcar conductor in Peoria, Illinois. He had two children but before he and his wife celebrated their eleventh wedding anniversary she died. Left with a five- and an eight-year-old son, Levi took his boys, Russel and Cecil, back to Natrona for dear old Sarah Graffis to raise. Dear old Grandma Graffis! How she had been refined in the crucible of life. She had lost her husband, Abraham, and two of their thirteen children. Single-handedly she saw them all grow to maturity and leave her one by one. When Levi brought Cecil and Russel to her empty house she welcomed them. She would not need to work to support them but could have the joy of cooking and sharing her meals with them and again hear the voices of children in the house. She wept for Levi in the loss of his wife but rejoiced to hear again the sound of footsteps in the house.[2]

It pained her deeply when Runnion told her he was going to leave Illinois' quiet Green Valley and move far away to North Dakota's Red River Valley.

All through the months and weeks of their planning, Grandma Graffis grieved. Runnion was to leave first and prepare for the coming of Uncle Ben Perdue with the box car that would carry the farm and household goods and livestock.

A very quiet and sad May went to Natrona to stay with Grandma until Runnion and Uncle Ben had everything in readiness in North Dakota. Sarah Graffis had turned seventy-nine in January and she fondled eight-month-old baby Marshall in desperate love because in her heart she felt she would never see her grandsons again. Uncle Levi did his best to cheer the twins. He went to the store and bought five cents' worth of nails and found blocks of wood and gave the twins hammers to pound at will. He ordered his sons, Russel and Cecil, to oversee but not interfere with the budding carpenters.

When word came it was time for May to take her boys to North Dakota, Grandma Graffis was broken-hearted. She told them to fluff up the feather beds before they left and smooth out every body mark that would remind her of them. Uncle Levi would travel with May to mind the twins while May cared for baby Marshall. Cousin Russel, Uncle Levi's oldest son, was then thirteen years old and would be man of the house until his father returned.

Sarah Elizabeth Enyeart, first cousin and wife of
Abraham Graffis and mother of Runnion Graffis

Leister, being the older of the four-year-old twins, took charge of the collapsible tin cup which was to offer a simple diversion for the three-day train ride. As they traveled westward Uncle Levi followed the twins to the faucet and rest rooms as each twin took his turn on oft-repeated urgent calls. One amusement for the twins was to study the etchings Jack Frost painted on the train windows. They discovered all sorts of fairyland pictures as they lived day and night in their heavy winter clothing. May tried anxiously to shelter baby Marshall as she nursed and made needed changes all within the limited area available on the full train.

It was early in the morning when the conductor announced, "Next stop, Walcott." The twins, awakened from another cramped night of sleep, were happy in the assurance that they would soon see their daddy. Eagerly they helped gather everything together with Uncle Levi's guidance. Mother attempted to spruce them up as best she could in their travel-weary togs. There hadn't been any changes for them since Grandma Graffis had tearfully buttoned them warmly, three days before in Illinois.

The train came to a grinding halt. Uncle Levi led the way to the train steps and restrained the eager twins in their impetuous desire to reach their father. Runnion greeted the twins and then hastened to help May down the steps with baby Marshall. Spotting the old familiar wagon and horses, the twins bounded forward, eager to climb aboard.

May held baby Marshall close as the wagon lumbered along on the four-mile journey to their new home. She was filled with an overwhelming sense of homesickness and felt in her heart she would never feel at home in North Dakota. She looked out over the vast stretches of almost treeless countryside and yearned for the forested hillsides she left behind in Illinois.

Chapter Four
'Neath the Shade of the Cottonwood Tree

Things looked better as the horses turned into the quarter-mile lane that led to their new farm home. It was a comfort to May to see that the lane was edged with cottonwood trees. As they approached the farm buildings she recognized the pendant branches of willow trees here and there around the buildings and a large cottonwood tree standing protectively by the house.

How good to hear the driver's "Whoa!" and have the wagon stop by the front of their new home. The boys were all eagerness as they were helped off the wagon and directed to the door. How good it was to stretch! There was a warm fire burning in the kitchen stove and food simmering in familiar kettles. Leister and Lester hastened to throw off their heavy coats and look around. There was the family water bucket which suggested a drink. No more did they have to wait for their turn to drink from the old collapsible tin cup. By now they had warmed their toes and fingers near the kitchen range and were thinking of food. Mother made baby Marshall comfortable, and then they all gathered around the table for breakfast. It was fun having Uncle Levi and Uncle Ben around the table. How good it was to eat at a table again with both Father and Mother in their places.

May Graffis was justified in missing the woodlands of Illinois. By the nearby Red, Sheyenne, and Wild Rice Rivers there were trees. In other areas trees were limited largely to areas around the homesteads. Legend places the blame for this on the king of Sweden and Paul Bunyan. That king wanted to establish a new Swedish kingdom in North Dakota. He felt his people could not cultivate forested lands so he hired Paul Bunyan to clear away the trees and do it in one month.

Bunyan set up his camp to carry out the order. He brought such a large crew that he slept them in bunks eighteen feet high. He fed them in a dining room so large that the boy who drove the salt and pepper wagon would be only half-way round by nightfall. He would sleep at his stopping place at day's end and return the next day.

Bunyan was reported to have completed the job in one month, but the king of Sweden was not satisfied with the job. He said his people could not cultivate land with stumps everywhere. Johnnie Inkslinger saw that Paul Bunyan was stumped and offered a suggestion. Since Blue Babe hated getting his feet wet, the thing to do was to borrow several large fire hoses and flood the land. To avoid getting his feet wet, Blue Babe would walk on the stumps and drive them into the ground.

Paul Bunyan liked the idea, and Blue Babe roamed all over North Dakota on the stumps and drove them six feet into the ground. The king of Sweden was satisfied when he could not find a single stump in North Dakota.[1]

In reality the fertile floor of the Red River Valley had once been the bed of a glacial Lake Agassiz which had given the area a black silt soil twenty to thirty feet deep abounding in artesian wells and natural springs.[2] The rich deep soil seemed to be a land of promise to Runnion as he transplanted his family to the Red River Valley. He had high hopes of building a future there for his three growing boys. To both parents it seemed an ideal setting in which their sons could grow and learn a wholesome way of life.

When their first breakfast in Red River Valley country had been enjoyed the twins were intent on exploring their new world. They found their old sleigh and went to find the wood pile and revert to their old responsibility of bringing wood for the kitchen range. They discovered the pump and immediately wanted to learn to use it. They went with their father to the barn and learned where to find food for the horses, cows, and calves. There was a huge haymow in the new barn which was to be a favorite haunt for the remaining winter days. Father warned them to stay far away from the hay holes except when they were pushing hay down to feed the horses and cows.

By nightfall the two tired boys were scrubbed and outfitted in their nightwear and sent to their goose-down beds, at home again in the routine of family life.

Very soon signs of spring appeared. The tawny stubble fields turned green with new growth of mustard, tumble weed, pasque flowers, and myriads of other wild plants. The meadow larks saluted the spring with their whistled slur, "Spring is here." The red-winged blackbirds joined with "o-ka-lee, cong-quer-ree."[3] Warmer days gave the twins freedom to explore. It was fun watching the blackbirds, who claim the Red River Valley as their own. Flocks of them followed father's plow, intent on getting grubs or insects turned up by the plow. Their days were colored with the beauty of North Dakota sunrises and sunsets, the dew halos that formed around the sun and moon, and after a summer shower, rainbows that came at times in perfect duplicate and triplicate gleaming arcs.

Their quiet world was filled with many voices of nature. There was the call of the coyote, the chatter of the flicker tails, and the crowing of the roosters at day break. As they wakened in early dawn on spring mornings they were greeted by the pre-dawn symphony of birds serenading their mates.

They were busy from dawn till dusk. Even at an early age there were many contributions they could make to the family. They carried water to the garden when Mother was planting. The kitchen water bucket needed to be refilled at the wooden pump, and they watched that the water trough for the animals was kept filled. As they fed chickens, pigs, cows, and calves they became soul partners in the family enterprise.

In keeping with an old adage, "All work and no play makes Jack a dull boy," Father and a hired man took time out to arrange a swing for the boys. They securely tied a strong rope to one limb of the cottonwood tree that overshadowed the house. The boys loved their swing and pretended they were sailing through snowflakes when the cottonwood seeds ripened and sent their white fleecy seeds like snowflakes everywhere. Sometimes Mother would come out and push them on the swing and recite to them part of Robert Louis Stevenson's poem:

"How do you like to go up in a swing,
Up in the air so blue?
Oh, I do think it the pleasantest thing
Ever a child can do?"

May Perdue had never been able to attend school beyond the fifth grade. As soon as she was old enough she had been hired out to help support the family. She was very sensitive about her lack of schooling, especially after she married a school teacher. She was intent on learning and became as knowledgeable as any college graduate. Going for the mail was a big event in the day. Would there be a magazine for Mother with the next chapter of that exciting story she read to the family last month? May subscribed to many magazines, some of which carried continuing stories, which she read to the family at day's end.

To go for the mail they needed to cross the lawn of their Norwegian neighbors, the Albert Bakko family. The twins liked making advances to the Bakko turkeys, which wandered at will not only in the Bakko farmyard but also into the Graffis yard and garden. The coffeepot was always on the stove in the Bakko kitchen, and there always were special homemade Norwegian dainties to enjoy when on occasion the boys had permission to stop in at their kitchen. This was a rare treat as the children were given strict boundaries.

As winter approached the wood was stacked in preparation for the snows that would surely come. Sundogs appeared in the sky as omens of winter weather. Straw and manure were packed around the cold sides of the house to save heat and shut out cold drafts. Packed down with snow, this gave the house insulation against North Dakota's harsh winter winds.

All their neighbors were Norwegians. May was amazed at their cordial and generous spirits. On all sides of their home lived Bakko families. There were Willy, Henry, and Andrew on one side and Ollie and Helmer Bakko on the other side. Just before Christmas the mailbox neighbor, Albert Bakko, asked Runnion to come over and pick out a turkey for their holiday meal. This was unthinkable boldness to May and Runnion. Mr. Bakko insisted and when Runnion hesitated he focused on one of the largest turkeys, shot it with his twenty-two, and gave it to Runnion.

Albert Bakko's family had been original homesteaders on their lands, so Albert had gotten his ownership by inheritance. Christmas among these people was a new cultural experience for Runnion and May. True to Norwegian tradition all the Bakko kitchens were in a bustle from the beginning of December, preparing for the customary week of feasting between Christmas and New Year. *Kringles* and *Sandbakkels* were stored away in abundance. Bread and rolls known as *Julekaka* and *Julebullar* kept coming out of their ovens. Goat milk, *Gjetost* and liver paste, *Leverpastej* were stocked with dozens of other varieties of dainties, all stored away in anticipation of the coming festivities.

The Norwegian community would spend a full two weeks visiting back and forth, now here, now there, with singing, dancing, and feasting. Their love for music was expressed in singing with accordions, violins, and dancing. There was even an eight-stringed Hardanger-type violin in the neighborhood. The Graffis family was invited to join the neighbors, but since community folk always conversed in Norwegian they responded only occasionally to the hospitality.

Christmas was a very special day with the big turkey. There was a brand new brightly colored rocking horse chair for baby Marshall. He was a very active child and unlike the twins could not be placed on the floor with a toy and be found there for any length of time. He was very up-and-going, and May was happy to have the two older boys to watch him. The rocking chair hopefully would help contain him. For the twins there were simple toys, among them the then popular jumping-jack.

The twins never attended first grade. They were taught to read and were given their first grade basics by their father and mother. Beyond the basics the boys learned responsibility and worthy home membership. They knew that the night before washday, Mother needed the wash boiler filled with water. She would add lye to the water in the copper boiler so that in the morning she could skim off some of the minerals that made the water resist soap. After the wash tubs were emptied and the clothes all on the line the tubs needed to be cleaned thoroughly in readiness for the Saturday night baths. Everybody looked forward to Saturday as the day when the family went to town to shop and catch up on community news. In the summer months this excursion was taken in the evening, but during the winter months it was a Saturday afternoon affair. This was the time to meet your neighbors, exchange views, and discuss community, national, and international interests.

Occasionally one or both of the boys would travel with their father to the bank at Colfax where Father had borrowed money to purchase his quarter section of land and farm equipment. At times it seemed Father was troubled after he came from the bank.

When Leister and Lester were sent to school they were greeted by Evelyn Hendricksen, teacher of Colfax School Number Four. The boys were able to begin public school in the second grade. The frame school had a large stove with a metal frame about it. It was to be a warm friend for the boys as Leister was to miss only three days in all the years he attended grade school. The blown snow, sometimes three feet deep, was so heavily packed that the children were able to walk on top without sinking, so snow, sleet, rain, or wind were never used as reasons not to go to school. Lunches were carried in gallon-sized Karo pails. There was no indoor plumbing, and drinking water was carried from the nearest well in the neighborhood.

Election time was always a big event in the family schedule. Father was a clerk of the election board and would be out most of the night on election days. Father also served as township clerk. He had beautiful handwriting, and the boys enjoyed watching him do his book work.

Leister had his first ice cream cone when his thirteen-year-old cousin Russel came to live with them. Russel was an adventurous boy and had gotten himself into disfavor with a man in his home community. Fearing reprisal, Uncle Levi sent Russel out to live with them to help with the work and avoid any further problem. It was this cousin Russel who bought Leister his first ice cream cone.

Gladys, Leister, Lester, Marshall, and Perry Graffis.
Taken about 1918, Gladys and Perry are children of
Uncle Elmer "Charlie" Graffis

"Grandpa Eillengson," a Norwegian neighbor,
and Gladys, Lester, Marshall, Perry, and Leister Graffis

16

Chapter Five
The Chameleon Valley–Oversold

During the Civil War, Jay Cooke of New York had so successfully promoted the sale of United States bonds to finance the Union Army that he became the leading banker in America.

After the war he became banker promoter for the Northern Pacific Railroad. Before he had consented to promote the railroad he made an extensive study of the Red River Valley. He called it "The Nile Valley of North America." He launched an international promotion of the area, making extravagant reports of the utopia that the Red River Valley offered.

He sold millions of dollars worth of bonds to Hollanders, and by 6 June 1872 the first Northern Pacific train crossed the Red River. Now that Cooke was ready to "bring in the sheaves, the Chameleon Valley put its worst foot forward."[1]

The summer of 1872 was so hot and dry that by August the prairies were burned a dingy brown and the soil was baked like granite. In September prairie fires turned the brown to black, exposing bleached buffalo bones.

In the next fourteen months only a few small tracts of land were sold. America's leading banking house, which had invested $30 billion in six hundred miles of Northern Pacific Railroad, was forced to close its doors. The Northern Pacific Railroad went bankrupt. Wall Street experts blamed the resulting panic on the worthlessness of the Red River Valley land offered as security for the Northern Pacific Railroad.

The following summer a cloud of grasshoppers settled on the Red River Valley, and all but the stubbornest settlers left the valley. This appeared to be the final curtain for the Fargo Land office that had hoped to promote the sale of the railroad land grants.[2]

One farmer had purchased forty acres of land from Mr. Powers, Land Commissioner of the then defunct Northern Pacific Railroad. In August of 1874 that farmer came to Fargo with sixteen hundred bushels of number one hard wheat for which he got the unprecedented price of $1.25 a bushel.

Word of more such harvests spread over the country. Men figured out forty bushels of wheat from single acre; a quarter section of 160 acres would yield $8,000; a full 640 section would yield $32,000; Red River Valley was better bonanza than California gold.

New developers emerged. Large investors called bonanza farmers came with as many as 150 gang plows and reapers. Fall threshing yielded two train loads of wheat daily from Minneapolis and a steamboat every other day from Duluth. The Dakotas' "Valley of Two Thousand Bonanzas" was a world wonder.

Land prices escalated, and fraud became epidemic. Small farmers who could not compete and eastern states finding the wheat growing center had been shifted from them to the obscure Red River Valley appealed to the press. The *Atlantic Monthly* warned that, if not curbed, the bonanza farmers would destroy American agriculture. Red River editors wrote about snow one hundred feet deep, railroads pulling up their tracks, people dying everywhere, wind tearing up great layers of earth, horror, terror, grim death hovering over the land.[3]

17

But they might have saved their newsprint. Fabulous legends of the bonanza harvests had been broadcast in America and Europe. Land values rose from between 60 and 70 percent, and there was a veritable stampede of Americans, Canadians, and Europeans to the valley.

Falling wheat prices and the droughts induced the Red River millionaires to incorporate into land companies and divide and sell. For the new managers of the reviving railroads life became a continuing basket of gold.

"The small farmers lured by the extravagant claims for the valley gambled their lives against great odds for great stake."[4] Runnion and May Graffis entering the scene in 1914 were confronted with those odds. The Chameleon Valley gave them one good season followed by a sequence of crop failures. One fall the owner of the farm came to see about his share of the crop. When he saw the devastation continuous rains had brought he told Runnion to keep for himself the little gleaned.

When Abraham Lincoln signed the Homestead Act in 1862 opening thousands of square miles of free land to anyone regardless of citizenship, homesteading began. Anyone who could convince the government he had lived on the land for five years could get the final deed to 160 acres, for the simple fee of $18 for a filing grant. That actually amounted to about eleven cents for an acre.[5]

The Civil War was to slay hundreds of potential farmers in the States. The Homestead opportunity was actually to have its greatest impact across the Atlantic.

Norwegian farmers having been exposed to negative reporting on the Red River Valley, had come as far as Minnesota but refused to enter the Red River Valley.

The promoters of the Red River Valley, wanting to lure these industrious Norwegian immigrants to the area, sent out an agent to search the valley for habitable areas. Before the agent had reached the valley he became an enthusiastic promoter and returned to declare "God gave the people of Moses the fertile Valley of Canaan. To us of Norway He has given the greater more fertile valley of the Red River of the north.[6]

A collapsed economy in Norway plus a shift in the migration paths of the herring, which took them away from their fishing grounds, made the news of the fertile Red River Valley like a utopian dream. Soon scientific methods were increasing production far in excess of demand.[7]

The Gold Era ended abruptly. The years 1920 to 1933 were depression years for agriculture. Low farm prices, floods, drought, dust storms, disparity between farm prices and non-farm prices caused Mr. Dyke, the Bakko families, and many of their neighbors to lose their farms. This cost-price squeeze, in which they purchased their needs at retail price and sold their products at wholesale, did not give them fair return for their products.[8]

Runnion Graffis, due to the malaise of the times, lost the 160 quarter section he had purchased and was forced to shift his family from one farm to another five times in a few short years.

Chapter Six
Commencement

As Leister worked side by side with his brothers as full partners in the family's joys and trials, they became bonded by a strong sense of family which would influence Leister's life style and loyalties as long as his parents lived.

The garden and farm stock, even in the leanest years, assured them daily food. Through her magazine, May kept pace with any innovations in food preservation and was one of the first homemakers in the area to cold pack foods. She gladly went out from her home to help neighbors and friends learn to cold pack. All the family worked together in harvesting and canning and helping to carry the Ball-sealed jars down into the cellar.

At an early age Leister demonstrated an intense interest and aptitude for things electrical. The postman's arrival was prime time for the family. The daily paper gave them a window on the world. When it carried a do-it-yourself feature on building a crystal radio set Leister was fascinated. His light remained on until early in the morning and he was really "charged" when at two in the morning the Sears Roebuck station WLS came through on his crystal invention. With a set of earphones, that little battery set was to keep this farm lad in touch with a larger world.

Work was always a priority. The boys never tried to "cop out." There was no whining, pampering, or rebellion for in their minds this was the only known way of life. All felt a deep sense of partnership and accountability in every farm concern and with unforced spontaneity and initiative, assumed their share of the responsibility.

There wasn't anything morbid about their family life. There were indeed shared anxieties, but with them there was fun and laughter that sometimes approached naughtiness. There was the time they teased the ram and roused him into a bucking temper. They lured the agitated sheep on to the creek full speed ahead. When they neared the creek they would quickly step aside and the charging ram would plunge head on into the creek.

At another time Leister had hooked up a live wire. He noticed one of his brothers riding toward him on Brownie. Now Brownie was the old mare whose pace had matured into a deliberate plod and was considered safe for anyone to ride. When Leister saw his brother riding toward him he touched the old mare's nose with that live wire. The gentle old horse lost all deliberation as she dashed toward the barn. Only the lower half of the Dutch stable door was opened, making entrance possible for old Brownie but not for her rider. By the mercy of the Lord the rider was spared serious injury in the brush-off.

Runnion had been living on a farm owned by Mr. Dyke. At the end of the war the owner wanted the farm for a brother returning from military service, so Runnion was forced to move his family out from under the shade of the cottonwood trees. For the next years they lived in areas near the Barrie Congregational Church, and Runnion and May led their family in church-orientated relationships. It was in that church the boys were to have their first extended Sunday School experiences, first in Aunt Florence's class and later in Uncle Vivian's class. Strong spiritual leadership at home, strengthened by Uncle Vivian's teaching, inspired Leister to make a commitment of his life to Christ. He gave first public expression to that faith by baptism in the Sheyenne River near Walcott.

The work routine of farm life did not deny to them participation in community and church activities. Barrie Congregational became the family church to the Graffis household. Every June all the church people united to make the annual picnic the crowning social event of the year. There was food galore emerging from the ladies' kitchens. Picnic tables were loaded with gallons of baked beans, potato salad, homemade cakes, pies, and breads. After the feast there were games for everyone such as sack races, three-legged races, potato relays, and volleyball.[1]

Runnion and his sons were all at hand for the baseball game. He had never lost interest in sports ever since, at the State Normal School in Normal, Illinois, he had helped his team take the football championship from Northwestern. Ball playing was by no means limited to the annual Sunday School picnic. Long before they had become part of the Barrie Church family, Runnion had played ball with his sons and community men and boys. Leister learned to coordinate with his father's own special curve ball so well that he became a regular catcher.

The Graffis family may have had the callused hands of farm laborers, but they were by no means just "dirt farmers." Besides a spiritually and academically oriented home atmosphere, they extended their interests outside the family. Runnion took his boys to programs scheduled by the Barrie Men's Club. There they heard lectures on such current issues as the "Teapot Scandal" and ethics of war. It was at the Barrie Men's Club that Leister first heard music of Chopin played by Miss Sharp from the Fargo Conservatory of Music. He loved classical music but also enjoyed hearing Betty Sheldon interpret on her violins such contemporary favorites as "Souvenir" and "Roses of Picardi."[2]

The Graffis brothers at an early age showed an aptitude and love for music. Though their mother May never learned well enough to play in public, she was able to find a melody on their reed organ. Leister was endowed with a musical ear that enabled him to learn to play the organ without formal lessons. He taught himself from a music manual on the family book shelf. Marshall had an excellent voice and began to sing publicly at an early age and eventually became part of the musical team. Leister was able to play the organ for the song times in the one room school he attended. Theirs was a rich full life which endowed them with character resources that would equip Leister for excellence in all he attempted in life.

There was a blush of dawn in the east as Leister walked toward the gate to bring in the cows for the morning milking. This was a special day, his graduation day from the eighth grade of Viking School. He was preoccupied with thoughts of all the day would bring. He only half noticed a robin tugging at a worm to carry to his fledglings. The dew was cool on Lester's feet as he guided the cows to the watering trough. One by one they took their places in the barn. While he milked the cows he rehearsed over and over in his mind the speech he was to give at the Viking School that evening.

Preoccupied in his thoughts he still was aware of the cats that waited with mouths ready. He would pause in his milking rhythm to send a spray of warm milk toward their open mouths.

When the last cow had been milked and the herd returned to the pasture, Leister turned the handle of the cream separator. The boys carried the skim milk to the hogs, who grunted and shoved as they slurped their milky way to "pork-i-ness." The cats sat in the morning sun licking their paws, using them to clean the whiskers of the misty milkiness they got from the udder fountain as the boys hurried to the house for breakfast. With family routine fully accomplished the boys dressed and prepared for school.

Each boy picked up the Karo can into which his mother had packed their last lunch for this school year, and the last lunch Leister would ever carry to public school.

The boys walked, whistled, and raced the two miles to school. Already the sun was high in the sky. By nine o'clock they were all in place for the morning routine of flag salute, Lord's prayer, and song time. There would be a rehearsal of the evening program, and then all the books would be stored for the summer and the whole room cleaned and decorated for the evening commencement program. Since they would be returning again in the evening the teacher dismissed them early.

One by one that evening the horses and wagons traveled toward the school. Leister and his brothers proudly escorted their parents to a seat near the front of the room. Runnion and May didn't think of the discomfort of being crammed into the school desks as they listened to the program and to Leister's commencement speech. While they joined heartily in applauding him they carried in their hearts a conflict of emotions. There was empathy for Lester who had not passed the eighth grade examination. His eye defect was more severe than Leister's, and he would need to return to Viking School for another try the following year. On the other hand, there was regret May and Runnion felt in the knowledge that they would not be able to send Leister on to high school. Family finances made it necessary to send their eighth grade graduate out to find employment to supplement the family income.

Chapter Seven
Toiling Upward in the Night

"Heights by great men reached and kept
Were not attained by sudden flight
But they while their companions slept
Were toiling upward in the night."

from "The Ladder of St. Augustine" by H.W. Longfellow

Leister's first job at the age of thirteen was cultivating corn on a nearby farm. The monotonous clumping of the horses lumbering feet as he "geed" and "hawed" them from dawn to dusk did not dim Leister's electrical aspirations. When the corn ears hung heavy on the stalks he worked with the huskers from sunrise to sundown and watched wistfully as he saw children returning to school. The monotony only intensified his determination to continue his education someday and become an electrical engineer.

When he got his first pay he walked home five miles to hand the full sum of his three-dollar-a-week pay to his parents, happy and proud to be able to contribute. As seasons changed he would sometimes earn as much as a dollar a day doing a man's work in such rush periods as hay and grain harvest times. Although the years of Calvin Coolidge's residence in the White House were considered good times for the country at large, there was a disparity between farm and non-farm income. The average American then was earning $750 a year while the average farm income was only $273. It was a time when a pair of overalls could be purchased for $1.25 and a pair of shoes for $2. Any money beyond his clothing costs Leister continued to give to help his parents.

After a year, Leister saw clearly that the family purse would not stretch to pay for any more public schooling for him. As he longed and prayed he came to the conclusion that if he was to have an education he would have to do it on his own. He decided on the American School of Correspondence because it did not demand an at-hand monitor of his study. The cost was five dollars a month, and he had to take a step of faith in embarking on the course that would cost him that much. The total cost would be $160 for sixteen credits. Farmers did not always pay monthly. Some waited until crops were sold so they could not assure him a regular income.

Pitching hay, gardening, herding, milking cows, and sawing wood from dawn to dusk left little time for study. Leister determined that regardless of the length of the work day or the level of exhaustion, he would spend at least fifteen minutes a day on school work. Again and again he would have to pay extra for extension of time on his schooling.

Despite his rugged routine Leister found time for sports and pranks. In baseball season he would walk home after Sunday morning chores to join his father and brothers in a neighborhood ball game. As the shadows would lengthen he would walk back to his employer's place to do the evening chores. In free moments he pursued every electrical opportunity that came into his path.

Finding an old magneto on a farmer's dump he reassembled it to make a live wire just for "kicks." With it he entertained the younger set at the farm with his own sideshows. They never tired of watching and chuckling as Leister touched his wire to the iron trough when a chicken came to drink. The feathered frenzy that followed filled them with fits of laughter.

Runnion Graffis purchased a threshing rig in partnership with another man. Threshing time was always a shared community event. The steam engine was fueled with straw because coal was too expensive. This meant the man who fired the steam engine needed to be up and ready to start the fires by four-thirty in the morning. By daylight the threshing hands were busy feeding, currying, and harnessing the horses. The belt needed to be put in place, the wagon wheels greased, and harnesses checked before the men ate a hearty breakfast to prepare them for the day.

Women were kept busy preparing food. There was breakfast for the early crew, noon and evening meals, and mid-morning and mid-afternoon coffee and sandwich breaks.

Leister spent free moments observing everything related to the steam engine. How he longed to operate it, but the partner who operated the steam engine was very possessive and jealously guarded his position as operator. Leister's secret ambitions found unexpected fulfillment when early in the threshing season the operator came down with appendicitis. Leister's twin brother, Lester, had been feeding the steam engine straw and now they were a team, keeping the engine operating; to Leister, barely in his teens, was given the responsibility of operating the engine for the period of the operator's convalescence. Leister gave thanks to the Lord for this opportunity for he saw it as a gift of an all-knowing Father who knew the desires of his heart.

The drudgery of dawn-to-dusk labor did not exhaust Leister's spirit. Music in his soul needed to find voice, and he hurdled every obstacle that stood in the way of expressing it. It was as a small boy accompanying his parents to the cultural events sponsored by the Barrie Men's Club that Leister's soul was stirred by the music of the masters. The Chamber of Commerce of the little village of Kindred, North Dakota hired a band director, a Mr. Huntley, to direct a community band. Leister purchased a used baritone and for four years contrived to get to a 9:00 P.M. band practice held once a week. This meant he would often have to miss his evening meal in order to complete his assigned chores in time to get to band practice. This director used only classical and military music. Soon the band was playing for picnics, civic events, and fairs. Their uniforms were white shirts and trousers, with the girls wearing white skirts and blouses.

Director Huntley resigned from the band to become head of the music department of the University of Nebraska, and the Chamber of Commerce hired a new director, Victor Picco, an Italian who had played the French horn in the Chicago Symphony Orchestra. When he first auditioned the band as its prospective director he told the Chamber of Commerce he would make their band a state champion in a year if he was hired. He was very demanding and expected undivided attention when he conducted. With one practice a week he went on to direct them to winning the state championship, taking it away from a band that had held the championship for two years and had had nightly practices preceding the competition.

What would have crushed the spirit of an average person only steeled Leister's determination and faith. When his employer offered him only the haymow for a bed, he used the solitude to plod on by kerosene lantern, working on his correspondence studies. When the drought that began in the summer of 1929 turned farm lands into scorched earth and made employment for him minimal, he still kept faith and plodded on toward his goal. When winter blizzards blinded visibility, he felt his way to the wood supply and in freezing cold did his part to secure a wood supply and keep his employer's family warm. While three-day blizzards raged he worked un-flinchingly, thawing out the pump and carrying buckets of water to the livestock in the barn.

During the Hoover administration and the crash of 1929 Leister's wages plummeted from fifty dollars a month to thirty dollars. Grateful for a job and food to eat, he milked as many as twenty-four cows at dawn and again at sundown after a full day of work.

By 1930 poverty became a way of life for forty million Americans. The drought that began in the summer of 1929 continued summer after summer. The subsoil was dust dry for fifteen feet below the surface. Cattle and horses died from starvation and from dirt they ate with the dried grass. Everywhere pastures were brown, with the plowed open fields literally lifted by winds that drove the dust into banks like drifted snow. Dust covered and penetrated everything, making house cleaning an endless drudgery. Machinery was ruined as the dust blended with the grease to grate and clog the operation. Farm after farm was lost to creditors.[2] Evicted farmers and farm hands wandered as migrants from Hoover Camp to Hoover Camp. These desperate, displaced people are graphically portrayed by John Steinbeck in *The Grapes of Wrath*.

Leister finally completed his high school education 5 December 1933, after ten years of self-study. The winter of 1932-33 had seen the most desperate months of the Great Depression. During the winter months when work was limited Leister still kept the welfare of his parents and brothers as a priority. Days and days were required to hand-saw enough wood to keep the household from freezing in winter. Sometimes the cold was so severe that some thin ice would form in the water reservoir attached to the kitchen range where all the family water was heated. One winter he assembled a gas-powered saw to cut wood for the family, thus assuring himself they would be provided for while he worked for others.

Chapter Eight
Academia

Twelve years as a farm laborer gave few opportunities for participation in church and civic activities. This lack of socialization did not enhance Leister's self-image, yet he never lost his hope of becoming an electrical engineer. Thoughts of entering college aroused mixed emotion. How could he, with his callused hands and correspondence school high school diploma, compete with younger more gifted students who had enjoyed the advantage of a formal educational experience?

In the midst of some of the most depressed times, Leister found employment just a few miles from Wahpeton and the North Dakota School of Science with George Wolfe, a former professor of chemistry at the State School. Although Mr. Wolfe served as county extension agent and was employed by the State Farm Loan Association, his first love was farming. He himself had owned several farms but lost all but one of them. He considered it a real indicator of the severity of the depression that he, with all his advantages, could not survive the disparity in economic opportunity that threatened agriculture.

Leister's employer, Mr. Wolfe, was the father of four boys, but that did not keep him from extending fatherly concern and sympathy for Leister's aspirations. In spite of the difficult years, this ambitious farm laborer had saved eighty dollars toward his college goals. Mr. Wolfe encouraged Leister to apply to the North Dakota School of Science. When President Riley reviewed Leister's application he suggested that he enter the trade school, as college policy ruled out accepting his correspondence school credits.

When Mr. Wolfe learned of the rejection he used his friendship with President Riley and Professors McMahon and Haverty. They had to admit that Leister was an anomaly. The mechanical drawings Leister had attached to his application reflected skills in advance of work required of their students. It was after careful deliberation and continued pressure from George Wolfe that the college conceded and gave Leister admission on a probationary status.

Leister prepared to enter in the fall of 1934 and to venture into his first experience in urban living. In preparation he needed to travel about thirty miles to his home at Walcott to collect his meager belongings. Although Wahpeton then had barely three thousand inhabitants, to this young country man this new life was threatening. When he had all in readiness to embark on this new adventure and had gassed up his old Model T, it balked. What a dilemma! He had been given that old car as settlement for a twelve dollar back wage owed him by a man unable to pay him.

Back in the days when he had worked for Ollie Bakko he had been able to save ninety dollars to purchase a 1923 Model Buick for his folks. He transferred his belongings to the trusty Buick. Seated on the plush red upholstery of the Buick, by his brother's side he was driven to his new life as a college freshman. There was no way he could afford dormitory life. He found a room to share with two other students at ten dollars a month, making each student's share a little more than three dollars a month.

Leister brought with him potatoes from the farm, the only contribution his parents were able to make toward his education. A man needed his automobile repaired. When Leister had made the repairs the man had no money to pay so he offered Leister a one-burner gas stove. The three students bought a table for seventy-five cents and were grateful for beans and potatoes for meals with corn mush for breakfast.

At that time only two students on campus owned cars, so this off-campus threesome took turns walking two miles to a place across the river that sold day-old bread at greatly reduced prices. The boys chose raisin bread when available and used peanut butter rather than dairy butter to save money. They carried the peanut butter sandwiches for their noon lunch, and although the better meals many enjoyed looked good to them, they did not waste time murmuring about their food.

Two other student brothers roomed in a nearby basement receiving free lodging there for caring for the furnace. These Wilbright brothers invited Leister and his roommates to use laundry tubs in their basement area to wash their laundry. In years to come one of the Wilbright brothers was to become a multi-millionaire as an entrepreneur in the manufacturing of hearing aids.

The first semester as a probationary student was a stressful experience. It had been ten years since Leister had been in a classroom. His eye defects impeded his reading speed. During those early weeks he lost seventeen pounds, but at semester's end he had earned all As and Bs.

To supplement his income, Leister got a job as shop assistant and "go-fer" for the head of the radio department at eight dollars a month. Professors Bill Haverty and Ben Barnard, head of electrical engineering, took a special interest in this highly motivated older farmhand student and did all they could to encourage and support him. Self-pity and resentment never colored Leister's emotions. Each advance in life he credited to the tender providence of his heavenly Father, never rescinding the early commitments he made to love and serve Him always.

While still employed with George Wolfe, Leister had become involved with the life of the Wahpeton Congregational Church. He found a church home there and was surprised to find even warmer acceptance in this urban church than he had enjoyed in the little rural church. He had anticipated that he, a country rustic, would be snubbed in an urban fellowship. He was truly surprised when a petite older lady, having overheard Leister's baritone singing, recommended to the choir director, Mrs. Paul, that she recruit Leister for the choir. He became a faithful, choir member for all the years he lived in Wahpeton.

When the school band director, Mr. Meyer, heard that Leister had been a member of the Kindred town band and had been trained under the direction of Mr. Picco, he at once offered Leister a place in the band. It was while playing with the college band that he came to realize what high quality training he had in the Kindred band. He realized, by contrast, the excellence of discipline and wealth of repertoire he had enjoyed in those early years.

In all the stress and tension of those difficult college years, there were times for fun and laughter. On days when band practice was scheduled, Leister would bring his instrument with him in the morning and store it above his locker until practice time. On one occasion as the band was performing to an audience, Leister just didn't seem to be able to hit the right notes. The band director looked askance at him. Perplexed, Leister positioned his instrument to drain out moisture that might by chance have collected. When he did this a large pickle dropped out from the throat of his instrument to Leister's surprise and to the amusement of the spectators. He was to learn later that the credit for this embarrassing moment belonged to dear "Bones" Welch, noted for his pranks.

Besides singing in the choir, Leister was an active member of the Young People's Society of the Congregational Church. Having a natural timidity and seeing himself as a country hillbilly, he humbly appeared for auditions for a play the group planned to produce. To his amazement he was chosen for the lead role. To him this was incredible, that he, a country novice should be assigned such a role. The play was well received, and the youth group traveled more than thirty miles to perform the play both at Fergus Hall and at Fargo.

Near the college was the state school for Indian children. Some of the boys were sent to Sunday School. Leister was asked to teach a class of Indian boys. His heavy schedule kept him from planning extra outside activities for these boys, but the insight into Indian culture he gained from teaching that class was to serve him well in years to come.

Dr. Clarence Bateman, a graduate of Moody Bible Institute who later followed a medical career, was one of the key members of the Congregational Church. His wife was superintendent of the Sunday School. When she became ill the Sunday School drafted Leister to act as interim superintendent. All these roles offered to Leister were far above all he would have aspired to as a boy who, years before, had slept in a haymow and toiled slowly upward in the night toward a high school diploma.

During his second year in college he was given more hours of work in the radio department, and his wages increased to twelve dollars a month. One of the first activities in which Leister participated when he entered North Dakota School of Science was the oratory club. His first year in the club was uneventful and a sideline experience. The second year he made the finals in the oratorical contest. At that time he was influenced by the isolationists, and he wrote his oration on "The Price of Peace," a current issue of the times. In the audience was his former employer and friend, George Wolfe. Competing with Leister for first place was one of Mr. Wolfe's sons. Leister was sure the Wolfe boy would take the top honor. When the judges awarded first place to Leister Mr. Wolfe was most gracious as he congratulated Leister. He rejoiced to see the confidence he had placed in Leister justified. Leister's heart was filled with gratitude for the honor he had not expected to win.

Graduation came, and Leister received his diploma in 1936. Jobs were scarce, and there was no prospect of employment for the new graduate. Leister packed his belongings and prepared to return to his early role of an ordinary farm laborer.

Marian Ammann (far right) as she traveled from the family homestead
where she was born to first grade in Montana with her cousin Roy
driving and caring for the horse at school.

Chapter Nine introduces Marian Ammann, who will in first person tell the rest of Leister's story as the one best qualified to tell it.

Chapter Nine
Patience of Love

The providence that had brought Leister Graffis to what seemed a blind alley in his life had not abandoned him. The same loving Father that was charting his course was also piloting mine. I, too, knew the hardships of displacement, depression and dust bowl. As a child, I lived with my parents on a homestead twenty miles north of Billings, Montana. Dorthea and August Ammann named me, their first-born child, Marian, and gave me every kindness they could afford.

When it was time for me to start school they had me vaccinated early in the year so that by school time it was all healed. Mother found a Karo pail for my lunch and grudgingly prepared to send me to school. Daddy felt the one-and-a-half-mile distance to the school was too far for a little five-year-old girl to walk alone, so he asked my uncle if his son, cousin Roy, could come and live with us to help with the chores and drive me to school in their two-wheeled cart. Roy could take me to school, drive and care for the horse during the school day, and bring me home again. I vaguely remember that day in September 1923. I already knew my alphabet and was eager to learn.

What Mother and Dad were unable to give me in material things they compensated for in protective love and caring. They had come to Montana in 1914 as newlyweds and invested their joint inheritance of four thousand dollars in developing a homestead. Year after year Dad planted in hope, only to see his seedling crops wither away, scorched by drought, heat, and wind-driven dust. Summer after summer he had to buy hay to keep his animals alive, borrowing money in hope that at harvest time he would be able to pay it back again. Again and again his harvests were barely enough for survival and the interest on his ever-increasing debts.

Finally in 1926 he gave up, sold all his farm stock and equipment to clear his debts, and determined to abandon his homestead and look for greener pastures. The returns from the sale of his equipment and stock just covered his debts. In deep embarrassment he asked the bank to lend him fifty dollars to finance a move to Minnesota. He kept the bare necessities in furniture and shipped them ahead to Fargo.

As a young man, my father, August Ammann, had spent some time in the Red River Valley near Fargo. There he had worked as a threshing hand for a man named Ben Willard. He recalled the lush green country and decided to go back to the Red River area of Minnesota to see if that old employer was still there and attempt make a new start in greener fields.

Our dog Nig and I walked back and forth in the park while Mother and Dad pitched our tent. Finally Mother called us to the picnic table where she had prepared a meal having used a little gas camp stove. Nig waited wistfully by my side for little morsels I would slip to him. Dad insisted that Nig must never be taken off his leash while we traveled. I learned the wisdom of that when during our walk, a rabbit dashed out of the grass. It took all the strength I had to keep him from taking off after that rabbit. At times I needed to tie Nig and care for my baby sister Ruth while Mother and Dad were busy around the camp. She loved to take my hand and go for short walks.

It had been a long, tiring day, and it was good to see a gleam of sunlight break through the clouds. The trusty old Model T, with many oil fills, had brought us thus far on our sojourn into the unknown. Like Abraham of old, Dad "went out" from Montana "not knowing wither he went." (Hebrews 11:8) Years later I recognized in John Steinbeck's graphic story *The Grapes of Wrath* a chronicle of my own life in retrospect. We were just one more migrant family displaced by contrary winds and the farm depression. It was a test of faith for Dad and a demonstration of loving patience for Mother.

We had stopped that Wednesday at a park near Jamestown along U.S. 10. Traffic moving west reported the roads ahead were next to impassable. The rains had turned the clay into tacky gumbo that would bog down the tires and wheels in a hopeless mire. We hoped by morning the roads would dry enough for us to proceed.

The next morning Mother arose early to prepare breakfast while Dad broke camp and packed everything back into the waiting Ford. There was only a small place for Nig and me. I loved my baby sister Ruth, but having been an only child for six years, I could not help feeling a sense of displacement when Mother needed to reserve her lap for Ruth, and I suddenly needed to share Mother with another.

The exodus that began on Monday in Montana ended Saturday when we came to Fargo. Dad's first move was to try to locate Ben Willard. He was relieved to find him still living in the area. He made room in his already full household for us. He soon located a vacant house, and we were given permission to live there. Birds had been the only residents of the house for several years and had flown in and out of the broken windows in unchallenged proprietorship. Mother bravely took over, evicted the birds and their droppings, and made it livable with almost no resource but her own ingenuity.

When we packed in Montana there had been no room for toys. Mother did find space for a shoe box of petrified fossils she had collected from the old lake bed in Hoskins Basin. Those fossils were to provide me with many moments of entertainment as I studied them and tried to guess what they had been.

Our new neighborhood was a most compassionate one. With our neighbors' help and with hard work, Dad was gradually able to rebuild his life. In the midst of the struggle, while we actually had only one large furnished bedroom, a third daughter arrived 29 May 1927. Though provisions were meager for four and we were heavily taxed to make room for a fifth, this sister, Velma, said in later life she never felt neglected or unwanted.

During my last years in grade school I was able to help my little sister Ruth get her start in school. Despite the hardship, Mother was determined that I should have a high school education. The nearest high school was in Wolverton, fifteen miles away, and there was no available bus transportation. The only person Mother knew that lived in Wolverton was our mailman. She steeled herself enough to appeal to him for help. Would he need a girl to do housework for room and board? He consented to give me a chance. For half the school year I lived with his family and for the second half with a minister's family. I was helped to find board and lodging for the three remaining years and was thus enabled to graduate from Wolverton High School.

In all their hardships, my parents always tithed, and the Lord in His faithfulness did supply our needs. Mother's dreams for me to have a college education were suddenly fulfilled when my aunt suggested she lend me money to attend North Dakota School of Science the next fall to be a companion to her own daughter entering that college in September. My parents both were grateful for this provision, and in the fall of 1936 I began my first experience of college life.

I was young and eager for life and made friends easily. Mother and Dad had always made the church central in their lives and in keeping with my training I attended the Congregational church nearby and became active in their youth group.

That youth group included a very active member who impressed me. I noticed him everywhere. When I went to a ball game there he was playing a baritone in the band. When I looked over the course offerings, there he was teaching a class in trigonometry. I went to Sunday School and there he was teaching a class of robust junior-age Indian boys. He mystified me. How could one person be so many places? I came into closer contact with him when I went to English literature class. There he was as a student with the rest of us. I began to ask about him to try to probe the mystery of his multiple roles. An article about him appeared in "Campus Faces" and I searched that for clues. I discussed him with the girls and was a bit shaken when one of the girls boldly announced that she planned to date that guy. I hoped in my heart I would win out over her.

I found my heart becoming more and more involved. As I sat in church my eyes wandered constantly away from the speaker to where this mystery man, Leister Graffis, sat in the choir. As the choir sang I fancied I was able to hear his rich baritone voice, and it put a song in my heart. I learned that he was a graduate student who had been invited to return for a third year and work as an assistant teacher. He had returned because he wanted to take some liberal arts courses not included in the two-year electrical engineering course he had completed. Most engineering students didn't elect English literature classes, but I was told he wanted the enrichment of this course. As I took in his responses in class I was even more enamored.

My dreams suffered a jolt when my aggressive classmate announced the fulfillment of her avowed purpose. She had a date with that handsome third-year guy. As I sat in my room that night, I hoped and hoped she would lose out in her pursuit. She came back elated, but days and weeks passed, and she never mentioned another date.

Meanwhile I was meeting him casually in the youth group at church. One crispy winter evening the group went on a sleigh ride. My heart kept pace with the horses' hoofs and tingled with the sleigh bells as we sat in the same area of the sleigh. The family that hosted the group to hot chocolate and cookies had a daughter who was very open about her designs on Leister. Was it in self-defense or to underscore his disinterestedness in her aspirations that he asked if he could walk me home? That walk was fuel to my emotions.

"How do I love thee?
Let me count the ways
I love thee to the depth
and breadth and height
My soul can reach."
                        Sonnet 43

Of all the poets that we studied in the English Literature class, none reflected the emotions growing in my heart like the sonnets of Elizabeth B. Browning. I asked my heart what it was that drew me to that elusive third-year student? I learned that he was the son of a poor farmer and that all his father could contribute toward his education was an occasional sack of potatoes. Somehow that only impressed me more. Here was one who had enjoyed even less support in his education than I, yet he had attained such a full life.

It was not until the last month of school that Leister actually dated me. He even took me out for ice cream sodas to top off our dates. I didn't know until later that he allowed himself this indulgence only after he was assured of a job at the State Training School in Mandan. The truth was that all this time he had no resources for dating, but after he had a job promise he borrowed twenty dollars from his brother and indulged his disciplined emotions in a month-long extravagance.

We discovered we both had the same convictions. Our parents had frowned on movies, so in respect for them we did not attend movies, and we didn't have to have money for church activities. These times we had together fed my emotions and again I borrowed from Elizabeth B. Browning to express their fervor:

"What I do
And what I dream include thee, as the wine
Must taste of its own grapes. And when I see
God for myself. He hears the name of thine.
And sees within my eyes the tears of two."
                        Sonnet 6

Too, too soon the final tests of the year were at hand and then came farewells. My aunt had not committed herself to help me for more than one year, and my folks would not be able to pay for another year of college for me. As I walked up and down the campus with friends I had come to cherish I tried not to spoil the magic of those hours with forebodings. I dared not try to guess what the next months would offer. My only prospect was to try to find a job to pay back my aunt and earn money myself if there was to be more college. We packed away our personal belongings and walked out of our empty rooms. It was hard not to shed a tear as I said goodbye to friends I might never see again.

As Leister and I parted he was totally non-committal about the future. He was charged with anticipation in the prospect of his first real teaching job. We would be miles apart I knew. When would our paths meet again?

"Go from me. Yet I feel I shall stand
Henceforth in thy shadow. Nevermore
Alone upon the threshold of my door
of individual life."
                        Sonnet 6
                        E. B. Browning

Chapter Ten
The Enigma of Love

"There are three things which are too wonderful for me,
Yea four things which I know not:
The way of an eagle in the air;
The way of a serpent upon a rock;
The way of a ship in the midst of the sea;
And the way of a man with a maid."
Proverbs 30:18, 19

Leister turned westward, and I turned toward the east. When would our paths meet again? He plunged into setting up a trade course for delinquent boys in the state correctional school at Mandan, North Dakota. Previously the school had offered only academic education. In organizing the trade courses Leister was guided by G. W. Haverty, the assistant state supervisor of trade and industrial education. Leister spent the summer organizing and purchasing equipment for a forty-by-ninety-foot shop. In this space he was to instruct approximately forty boys for at least three hours a day, five days a week, in automobile repair, gas engine operation, farm mechanics, and inside wiring.

W. F. McClelland, superintendent of the Mandan State Training School, hoped to provide every boy enrolled in the school with the rudimentary knowledge of some trade and to fit him for employment after he left the institution.

I unpacked my bags and returned to the diversified activity of farm life. Baking, weeding, feeding, and reading were all secondary preoccupations. My thoughts traveled westward, doggedly trying to visualize what Leister was doing as I waited for mail. I dared not write as often as my heart dictated. He wrote one week, and I answered the next, so we each had a letter about once in two weeks. His letters seemed so matter of fact in contrast to the depth of emotion that dominated my heart.

He was to be home for Christmas. I counted the days and hours. In our short time together he spoke freely of the boys and his family and seemed politely interested in all I had to say but never gave a clue as to the feelings of his heart. He left, and I was no more certain of his love than I had been after our dating extravagance just before we left college.

I felt crushed. If all he wanted was a casual friendship why suffer any longer? Perhaps all he needed was a little prodding. I labored over a letter, hoping if I suggested terminating our friendship it would bring an affirmation of love and a commitment to a more meaningful relationship. It didn't work. He did write and asked forgiveness for anything he said that had offended. I couldn't tell him it was what he hadn't said that was the problem.

Our bi-weekly letters terminated, and I wet my pillow many a night with tears. There was never a word exchanged until the next holiday and then only a card with his signature. He was totally involved with his boys at the school, the local Methodist church in Mandan, and his family. As a boy graduating from eighth grade he had gone to work cultivating corn. His first pay of three dollars was given in full to his parents. When he got his first pay for teaching at the training school he sent it to his parents to buy dentures. I respected his loyalty to his parents, but I also resented it. Why should a man of his age be so sensitive to the needs of his parents and so insensitive to love? In 1939 he actually purchased a three-hundred-acre farm for twelve dollars an acre for his family. He put the farm in his twin brother's name but made himself liable for the payment. At least thirty dollars a month from his $150 monthly pay check went for the farm payment leaving him little more than enough for bare personal needs.

I was to learn later that Leister was not immune to love but he felt there was no way he was prepared to assume responsibility for another person when he was barely meeting his own needs. Reason always dominated passion for Leister, and my letter left him puzzled. He related to other girls in courtesy relationships but never with the thought of a permanent tie. I participated in the social life of our church group without giving the image of a morbid spurned lover, but always my heart and thoughts were fixed on Leister.

Meanwhile I concluded, in spite of buckets of tears, that if ever I was to have a chance with Leister I needed to do something with my own life. My sisters Velma and Ruth were now in high school and for them bus transportation had become available. They could now take my place doing farm chores. I returned to college after a year to major in home economics at the Agricultural College in Fargo.

As soon as Leister was settled in Mandan he spent his Sundays attending church. He felt comfortable in the Methodist church, finding great inspiration from the ministry of its pastor, Dr. Wallace. He made himself available for any service need there might be in the church. Within a few months he was given a class of boys who were reported to have driven out three previous teachers. He came to enjoy the challenge and took the boys on trips to the airport, to see the flood waters of the Missouri River, and to his shop on occasions for little projects. While at Mandan he was to serve as an elder and Sunday School superintendent. As a farewell they gave him a beautiful large print Moroccan leather Bible, the first large print Bible he owned. In the presentation the pastor asked if anyone knew which was the only department of the church Leister had not served. No one could think till the pastor named the "Fifth Wheels," the name the Single Women's Group had given themselves.

There were Indian reservations near Mandan. Many of the Indians stopped by to see their boys who were incorporated in the school. They would often come there barely making it to the shop in old jalopies they had salvaged from some junk heap. Leister would get the boys to work on the old jalopies and get them in working order. His experience with his class of Indian boys back at Wahpeton gave him insights that helped him build rapport with the Indians at Mandan. One day one of the chiefs came and brought Leister an honorary membership to the Indian tribe. The leading of the Lord in each step of his life filled Leister's heart with thanksgiving, and he never ceased to marvel that he, a backwoods farmhand, should be trusted with all the opportunities for service that opened up for him in each step of his life.

Besides his work and church activities, he also served as an adviser for the National Youth Administration Training Program. As international tensions mounted in 1940 and 1941 Leister was asked to teach an evening class four hours a night to experienced tradesmen. To prepare these men for a step up in defense, he was to give them a refresher course in machine shop practice, arc, and oxyacetylene welding.

It was wishful thinking for me to believe summer vacations would bring Leister east. In the summers of 1940 and '41 he compulsively attempted to upgrade his skills by attending summer sessions at Colorado State College.

For financial reasons it was necessary for me to work a year between my second and third year of college. I worked as a maid in a private home to help finance my education. I was helped my third and fourth year by an opportunity to earn my board and lodging in return for a few simple household chores and constant availability as a built-in babysitter for little Lynn Lagerberg. Her parents became my lifelong friends and I became deeply attached to baby Lynn as I watched her grow from a two- to a four-year-old darling. Lynn was to grow into a beautiful young lady and marry a professor at the University of Colorado. She was found to have cancer at an early age and battled her way to complete recovery. In gratitude she is spending her life helping others who suffer with cancer through an organization known as "Cansurmount."

One Christmas vacation my family planned to spend the holidays in Iowa and wanted me to go with them. Thinking Leister would be puzzled by an Iowa postmark on my Christmas card I added a note explaining that I was going to Iowa. That little note was responded to in a manner which opened the way for a renewal of our letter writing.

Leister was working a grueling schedule. Teaching boys all day long and men until eleven o'clock at night in the defense classes was exhausting. Men whom he had trained in the evening classes went to Lockheed Aircraft in Burbank. As he received reports from them he became interested in exploring a new field. Prayerfully he made application to Lockheed Aircraft in the conviction that he did not want to spend all his life at the Training School. It would mean a cut in pay, for with his National Defense Training Classes he was earning a good income. He was still paying for the farm, but in a step of faith he responded to an opening given him at Lockheed and resigned from the Training School.

Before moving to California, he took time out to visit his family and stopped by to see me for less than an hour. It was the first time we had seen each other in years, and I was able to introduce him to the Lagerbergs.

He was employed as a precision assembler at Lockheed, working on a four-to-eleven swing shift. This gave him more free time than he had had for years at the Training School. He became involved in teaching machine shop practices three days a week for two hours a day in a National Defense Training Class sponsored by Lockheed Aircraft in the Burbank, California, high school.

The National Defense pressures made the area around Burbank congested. The only lodging available was a single room shared with two other men, with restaurants nearby. Again he found a friendly Methodist church to attend. He made himself available and soon was teaching a fine class of intermediate boys. His class had to meet in an Elks Hall near the church as the rush of wartime defense preparations had brought such an influx of people to the area that everything was crowded. The hall was used the night before for lodge activities and was cluttered with beer bottles and the day-after debris, making it necessary for the boys to set up chairs and prepare the area for class. These were among the finest boys Leister ever taught.

While still at the training school Leister had been exploring possible doors open to him. He had taken a Civil Service test for radio engineer. When he had not heard from them he saw Lockheed as an open door. He was not at Lockheed more than a few months when in March 1942 he was offered the position of Radio Engineer under Civil Service in the employ of the United States Signal Corps at the Presidio of San Francisco.

Since this was the area of his deepest interest and offered a more challenging future than Lockheed, he felt the Lord had opened another door for him. He was put in charge of the course instruction and lesson materials to be used for training radio and radar technicians in the universities and state colleges on the west coast. Besides writing materials he assisted in instructing the teachers who were to teach the courses.

During all these changes Leister did find time to write and tell me about the affairs in his life, but there was no real heart exchange in his letters. I longed and waited for some assurance that I was more than just another friend to him in a love that, as far as I was concerned, seemed "to suffer long." (1 Cor. 13:4)

Chapter Eleven
In Due Time

The colonel under whose command Leister worked at the Signal Corps recommend that Leister apply for a commission in the army in hopes that the army would then authorize his being retained at his desk right there in the Presidio. The army refused the commission on grounds of Leister's poor eyesight. The colonel, in his disappointment, then advised Leister to go to Treasure Island and apply for a commission from the navy. It was common knowledge that the navy was so desperate for radar technicians it was waiving physical handicaps for qualified men. It was faith in a God with whom "all things are possible" (Mark 9:23) that gave Leister the endurance to "try, try again." He had taken several Civil Service examinations in Mandan and had been rejected in all but the one with the U. S. Army Corps on the grounds of his physical handicap. The only thing that got him into the Signal Corps at San Francisco was their urgent need for men with knowledge of radar.

About that time word filtered back to Leister's home draft board in North Dakota that Leister had applied for a navy commission. Fearful that they would not be able to make their quota of recruits, they conscripted Leister and wrote on his conscription papers, "No limitations."

The staff at the Presidio banqueted Leister in a reluctant farewell. They were all there, even his efficient blonde secretary. The colonel gave him a letter of introduction recommending that he be assigned to the Signal Corps. That letter was a deciding factor in his assignment to Camp Crowder, Missouri.

Life as a buck private in the army was like a vacation to Leister, who had been working fifteen to eighteen hours a day at the Presidio. The day came when the new recruits at Camp Crowder were to have a workout on the rifle range. That was a welcome prospect to Leister who was anxious to get a gun in his hands again. He came from a long line of gun enthusiast, and he was eager for another chance to shoot target.

The second lieutenant, an ROTC man, called Leister to him and said, "Graffis, you will work in the barracks today. Your eyesight disqualifies you for rifle range duty."

Leister's response could have gotten him a court-martial. He had never used his eye defect as a reason for not participating, and he was not going to sit still and let it be used to keep him from his favorite sport. He spoke up, "My induction papers say, 'No limitations.' How can you exclude me?"

It was true that his draft board had written, "No limitations," but the saying among the recruits at that time was that as far as the army was concerned, if you were warm you were in. The second lieutenant was in touch with reality and had valid reasons for excluding Leister. The physical examination given him when he reported to Camp Crowder recorded that his vision was seriously impaired. Due to a congenital eye defect the sensitive cones in his eyes that gave acuity and color detection were lacking. His rods were normal, giving him good night vision.

Fortunately the second lieutenant was moved by Leister's intensity and permitted him to go to the range on probation. Out on the range as he waited in a long line for his turn, he observed that some of the men ahead of him had never handled a gun. He offered them assistance on how to handle, aim, and fire. When his turn came he made marksman. At the end of the exercise the drill Sergeant called Leister aside and gave him a paper for the second lieutenant requesting return the next day as an instructor.

When the second lieutenant got the request it must have been an enigma to him. He could not have known that the farm hand from Walcott, North Dakota, had been part of a father-son team that sprang from a family with a traditional obsession with guns. Leister's father had given him a 1912 Winchester on his twelfth birthday. Walcott's hinterland abounded with jackrabbits, prairie chickens, pheasants, ground squirrels, and coyotes. Hours of Leister's life had been spent waylaying the ground squirrels and gophers that would burrow the length of the corn rows to steal the corn.

Instead of indulging in pouting and resentment at being made a buck private, Leister retained his sense of humor and his ability to laugh. Leister and his comrades were some of the new recruits from the Santa Barbara, California, recruitment center who had recently arrived for army basic training prior to their assignment to specialized fields. Many of them were mature men, university graduates, and men experienced in high technology.

These new recruits were assigned to a platoon led by a youthful corporal, nineteen or twenty years of age, whose qualifications were based on his length of time in the army. This young platoon leader officiously chewed out his men as he barked out orders. The mud oozed around their boots as they maneuvered on the wet field. As the corporal marched backward on the drill field in front of his platoon he suddenly fell backward in the mud. This was too much for these older seasoned men, and some of them burst out in laughter. Recovering himself in bemuddled indignation, he ordered every man that laughed to K.P. duty for the weekend. Leister and his buddies were still chuckling as they traveled toward the mess hall. After all, a good laugh was easily worth one more potato peeling sentence. Actually the sentence to K.P. duty was just another relaxing fun time to Leister after the intense life he had lived in the past.

At a later reveille this same platoon corporal asked the men for volunteers for a scrub-up job at the newly finished FM Radio Headquarters building. Leister's sights were on that area, and he rationalized that he would get there if he had to crawl on his hands and knees. His platoon buddies looked askance at him when he volunteered. You just do not volunteer for anything in the army! No one else volunteered so the corporal drafted two others.

It was a steaming hot day. The three men stripped to their waists, and their bodies dripped with perspiration. While they were hard at it the captain in command stepped out of his office and came to where they were working. He asked if any of them could type. No one responded, so Leister stood at attention and said, "Sir, I have some typing skill." He asked Leister to report to his office.

Leaving his buddies, Leister went to the washroom, cleaned up, and reported to the captain. He was given a manuscript to copy. After typing for several hours he took the finished papers to the captain and said, "Sir, there were some errors on those papers, and I took the liberty to correct them." This sounded like a presumption, and the captain demanded an explanation. As Leister pointed out the corrections the captain recognized the validity of his corrections and asked how he, a buck private, knew how to make the corrections.

Leister replied, "Sir, I wrote those job sheets when I worked in Radio Engineering at the United States Army Signal Corps at the Presidio in San Francisco. I was working on those materials when I was drafted and I was aware of corrections that still needed to be made."

Now a buck private always stands at attention in the presence of a captain. The captain gave the order, "Sit down! Tell me who you are and what you are doing as a buck private with this kind of know-how."

Leister told him briefly about his life-long obsession with radio from his crystal set to his college experiences and work at the State School of Science. The captain broke in, "I want to hear more of this, report to this office Monday morning." As Leister returned to the barracks he was overwhelmed with the way the Lord honored his heart's desire to get into the FM Headquarters. Who could have dreamed of finding the right-of-way to the captain's office by way of a scrub bucket?

The captain was a first-generation Japanese-American and an ardent patriotic citizen of the United States. He was a graduate of Texas A&M and a licensed pilot. Because of Pearl Harbor all Japanese were kept in the background, so he had been sent to this inland base at Camp Crowder. When Leister reported to him Monday he said, "Graffis, you are the man I am looking for and I want you to set up our FM program here." The remarkable convergence of events that brought Leister forward at such a strategic moment proved to him, as it must have to the captain, that someone higher than chance was shaping Leister's ends. It was a cause for deepest gratitude to the Lord on Leister's part that he, a buck private, should be asked to pilot the whole program. When he voiced his apprehension about a buck private issuing orders to men of higher rank, the captain assured him he would take care of that.

When two trained sergeants arrived from Fort Monmouth, New Jersey, and were placed under his command he took refuge in an old favorite verse from Proverbs 3:5, 6: "Trust in the Lord with all thine heart and lean not unto thine own understanding. In all thy ways acknowledge Him and He shall direct Thy paths."

The captain kept his word. Within two weeks the announcement came at reveille that Leister Graffis had been promoted to private first class. In a few more weeks, promotions to corporal and then to sergeant were announced. All progressed well. His relationship with the two sergeants who took orders from him was compatible.

There was even time for letters. In the meantime I had graduated from college and had taken my first teaching position. I sent Leister one of my graduation pictures. He was not allowed to clutter the barracks with such distractions so he kept my picture in the bottom of his footlocker in the barracks. Mother was sentimental about "our boys" and felt folks should write to encourage them. I didn't need her encouragement for I still had my heart set on Leister. As he told of his dramatic rise to the top by way of a scrub bucket, I saw his life was a living proof of the admonition "Humble yourself under the mighty hand of God, that He may exalt you in due time. (1 Pet. 5:6)

Cpl. Leister F. Graffis
Camp Crowder, Missouri, 1942

Chapter Twelve
Letters End

"If you can dream and not make dreams your master;
If you can wait and not be tired by waiting
If you can meet with Triumph and Disaster
And treat those two imposters just the same
***
Yours is the earth and everything that's in it
And which is more–you'll be a man, My Son"
Rudyard Kipling

I was mystified. Less than four months ago I had erased the California address and replaced it with the Camp Crowder address. In his last letter Leister told how the whole platoon had lost their weekend passes. He explained that it is important to train army men in alertness, so directives are sometimes changed and merely posted. Every man is responsible to be aware. Regulations had been that shoes were to be lined up behind the cot post. A new directive ordered them lined up with tips straight with the post. Some of the men were caught with shoes in the old position, and the whole platoon lost their weekend passes. This had given him time to write a long newsy letter.

He had reported in the letter that he had gotten a second advance in his rating and was now a sergeant. That had been a very up-beat letter, telling his satisfaction in the solid foundation he was seeing laid for the radio maintenance school. He seemed so pleased that the staff under him were working so well with him. Now here was another letter with a third address from one L.F. Graffis, Lieut. J.G., United States Navy!

I hastened to open the letter. How could I account for what I found? He told me the whole platoon had gotten its shoes in perfect order and was all set for a weekend pass. After he left the office he stopped for his mail and to his amazement found a letter from the navy with the commission. He told how he returned to his Japanese captain. When the captain saw him he said, "Graffis, what are you doing here? I thought you had a weekend pass."

He explained how he laid the letter before the captain. He took it up, read it, and then got up from his chair, walked over to Leister, congratulated him, and said, "You are going to take it, aren't you?" This was above all that Leister had dreamed possible, for it is not the practice of the army to release men to the navy. So in a matter of months he had gone all the way from buck private in the army to lieutenant junior grade in the United States Navy.

THE

President of the United States of America.

To all who shall see these presents, greeting:

Know Ye, that reposing special Trust and Confidence in the Patriotism, Valor, Fidelity and Abilities of _____ LEISTER FINK GRAFFIS _____ I do appoint him _____ Lieutenant (junior grade) _____ in the Naval Reserve of The United States Navy to rank from the _____ Eighteenth _____ day of June 1942. _____ He is therefore carefully and diligently to discharge the duties of such office by doing and performing all manner of things thereunto belonging.

And I do strictly charge and require all Officers, Seamen and Marines under his Command to be obedient to his orders. And he is to observe and follow such orders and directions from time to time as he shall receive from me, or the future President of The United States of America, or his Superior Officer set over him, according to the Rules and Discipline of the Navy.

This Commission to continue in force during the pleasure of the President of the United States for the time being.

Done at the City of Washington, this _____ Fifteenth _____ day of September in the year of our Lord One Thousand Nine Hundred and _____ Forty-Two _____ and of the Independence of The United States of America the One Hundred and Sixty-Seventh.

By the President:

Frank Knox

Secretary of the Navy

112244

As I laid down the letter, I felt I was seeing the Word of God come alive, as there flashed into my memory the verse, "For promotion cometh neither from the east, nor from the west, nor from the south but God is the judge; he putteth down one and setteth up another." (Ps. 75:6)

I had been teaching my students in their home economics classes at Medina High School how to bake pumpkin pies. How I wished I could have sent one to Leister. We had hoped to see each other over the Christmas holidays, but now those hopes were all shattered. The navy had sent him to Tucson, Arizona, to a training center for navy officers. That was to be a two-month course, but before two months were over he was ordered to go to Boston for three months at Harvard and three months at MIT.

Since I would not see Leister over Christmas I spent my Christmas holidays making the best cookies in the cookbook and fixing them up in dainty cups with painstaking care. I mailed them with so much joy. He acknowledged them without too much praise and it was only years afterward that he told they were all crumbs when he received them.

The school year at Medina ran its course, and I returned to my home for summer, filled with excitement at the prospect of Leister's return after his course was finished at the end of June. I learned he would be arriving at his parents' home July 3, and I made certain I was there to greet him. We spent the day together and with his family. That night on the way home in his brother Lester's car, we sealed our engagement with a kiss. When we arrived at my home near midnight, I wakened my parents to tell them of our engagement. After that Leister stayed for another hour and then returned to his family.

Since Leister's leave was so brief and I had spent the whole day and half of the night in his company, Mother suggested I not go to the community picnic on July 4 but permit him that time with his family. I have never been certain if Mother advised me wisely, for he told everyone at the picnic that we were engaged and I was not with him.

The navy was sending him from Boston to Corpus Christi for Air Corps training before he would be assigned permanent duty. After Corpus Christi he would be sent out from Seattle, Washington. Leister said we would be married if he could get enough leave when he was moved from Texas to Washington. If not, I would go to Seattle over our Christmas vacation and be married there.

When the Japanese bombed Pearl Harbor my father made me a bet that the GIs would push the Japanese into the sea in six months. Six months had passed, so I called the bet on my father and used the hundred dollars for a trip to Corpus Christi to be near Leister for two wonderful weeks. I saved, sewed, and shopped for some good clothes for the trip, and we dreamed and planned together for our wedding day. The navy had said that Leister was not eligible for overseas duty because of his eyes, so we had hopes of soon being united for keeps.

School was soon to start, and the time for Leister's transfer from Texas to Seattle, Washington, was imminent. As soon as he was given his transfer orders he would let me know if he could get enough travel time to come home for the wedding. Sunday morning, 5 September 1943, I went to church in a drawn out state of suspense. On the way home from church we stopped at the depot. The wire was there! He would be coming home Thursday. In Iowa he would pick up Betty Strahorn, my college roommate. She would be my bridesmaid and her son, George, my ring-bearer. I wanted my little darling, Lynn Lagerberg, to be my flower girl, but her mother was ill at the time and would not send her with others.

I hurried to the church that evening and invited everyone to our wedding Friday, 10 September 1943. Our wedding day was the most fulfilling day of my life up until that time. We spent a week-end honeymoon in a Fargo hotel, then he was gone. I returned to teaching and waited eagerly to hear where he would be assigned to duty.

Marian Amman becomes Mrs. Leister Graffis   10 September 1943

We thought our days of separation would soon be over. Our love was again to have a lesson in patience. True, they did not send him overseas, but they did send him to a far-out island of the Aleutians as a radar officer for sixteen months, so again I lived from letter to letter. Now they were more frequent and there was no restraint in the expression of his feelings.

At the end of my second year of teaching in North Dakota I did not sign a contract for another year. I returned to my family in Minnesota and waited and prayed. I did not want to be bound by a contract should Leister be released. As I waited the Lord graciously supplied. One of the local teacher's mothers died. Her father was so grief-stricken they feared he would take his life, so she needed a leave of absence. It was the sort of opening I sought. By Christmas I was expecting Leister and just before Christmas she wrote to one of the other teachers and asked her if Marian wasn't soon ready to quit, as she was ready to return to her teaching position. To me it was the Lord's timing.

Letters End Aborted–Lieutenant Leister F. Graffis, loving again by letter.

Chapter Thirteen
Out of the Fog

I had taken the job teaching home economics in Mantorville, Minnesota, with the understanding that I would be free to leave when Leister returned from the Aleutians. We were approaching the end of the semester, and I felt it would not be fair to the children to have another teacher test them on material I had taught. I made and gave the tests and hastened to correct them. I even took them to ball games and accepted help from other teachers in my eagerness. As soon as I was free I packed my suitcases and set out for Seattle to be there when Leister returned.

Jim Moorehead's wife, whose name was also Marian, had taken residence at a boarding house in Seattle. Jim was Leister's favorite pilot, and he felt safest flying with him. She had come to stay in Seattle so she could see Jim whenever they returned to base for regrouping. I went to the same boarding place and found a room. She spent her time cooking for the navy men who passed through the base, so I occupied my time helping her. Day by day other navy men came and went, but there wasn't a word from Leister.

We weren't alone in waiting for they had been weathered in. They had started for Seattle but had encountered such heavy headwinds the pilot was doubtful that their fuel would last, so he turned back toward Anchorage. Leister's reputation as a sound sleeper and a real bird in his sense of direction was to be tested. When they reversed their course, Leister was sound asleep, strapped to his bunk. The men agreed not to tell Leister about their flight reversal and see if they could trip up his genius. When he awoke the first thing he asked was "Why have we turned back again?" Our joy was indescribable when he finally landed at Seattle.

Marriage by correspondence was over at last. Leister had orders to report to Cape May, New Jersey. On the way east we stopped to visit Leister's folks in North Dakota and to pick up my things and visit my folks in Minnesota.

When we arrived at Cape May the only lodging we could find was a single room with a hot plate. It was a beautiful resort spot, and here we were to enjoy an extended honeymoon at Uncle Sam's expense. I felt very indulged as I spent my days apartment hunting and sunning on the beach with the other navy wives. We finally located an apartment and from March to October 1945, our address was 219 North Street, Cape May, New Jersey.

Evenings were spent walking hand in hand on the boardwalk and sandy beach. Moonlight on the ocean, the music of the waves, all were conducive to dreaming and reminiscing. It was during these times together that I learned truths about his sixteen months as a radar officer on that farthest-out Aleutian island, Attu. Had I known the facts he shielded me from, I would not have slept so well or taught as well.

During that time, he told me he spent 996 hours flying–sometimes twelve hours at a time without seeing the wing tips of their patrol plane–searching for submarines and enemy planes and flying on bombing missions, much of the time with only instruments and radar to guide them. Fifty percent of the planes that went on bombing missions to Hokkaido, Japan, never returned, and none of the crews were ever found. They were lost not as often to the enemy as to the weather.

Adverse weather and losing the way in the fog caused them to run out of fuel, and for this reason they would fail to make it back to their base.

Life there was very lonely. He said some of the men would go berserk and have to be sent home in strait-jackets. The fog was so persistent that Attu was said to average only twenty-eight days a year when the sun was visible.

One day when Leister came home from the base at Cape May, he was chuckling. He had been to the airport in the morning and was puzzled at what he found. He had asked why there was no activity and when he learned all planes were grounded because of weather conditions, it seemed incredible to him. On Attu weather conditions like those would have been considered ideal for flying.

Even though we were at Cape May for less than a year, we found real identity with the people of the Methodist church there. We both sang in the choir and taught Sunday School. Leister taught older boys, and I taught junior boys. I had in my class the son of Reverend and Mrs. Everett Hunt. We built ties with the Hunts we knew were eternal. Years later when the Hunts celebrated their fiftieth wedding and ministry anniversary we were the only ones present from their early Cape May parish.

We were reluctant to become too emotionally involved with the people because we knew the time for Leister's discharge would soon come. This would end our paid honeymoon, and we would need to begin civilian life. A career in the navy was not Leister's option for many reasons. The regular navy would not accept anyone with a visual handicap as severe as Leister's. He had been accepted in the navy only because in a national emergency the navy had waived physical requirements for highly trained technicians. Leister was able later to remain in the reserves long enough to receive his full commander rating. Even if it had been possible for him to choose a naval career, he would not have done so. Leister had no desire to conform to a navy officer's life-style nor to be bound to the mobility one must expect in a naval carer.

In anticipation of his discharge Leister wrote his resume and sent it to about fifty prospective employers. Mail time was an exciting time in the weeks that followed. He had applied to such enterprises as Motorola, Philco, General Electric, RCA, Magnavox, and Bendix. As offers came he narrowed his interest down to two or three and began scheduling interviews. His first interest was Philco but when they suggested he might be sent to England he turned his focus to an offer from Bendix.

Finally in November 1945 he got his discharge from the navy. They gave him a ninety day leave with pay, so we decided to celebrate and travel westward to visit our parents. Leister also planned to include in our travels a visit to Motorola in Indiana. At Chicago he planned to stop at the Merchandise Mart where Bendix was showing their first models of home radios at a trade show there. At the trade show he contacted Don Kresge, who was then service manager for Bendix Radio. While there he finalized a commitment to a job offer from Bendix.

We traveled on to Minnesota and North Dakota, visiting our childhood haunts. My parents had never returned to the old homestead they had abandoned in Montana. We decided to travel with them to visit that site. We found someone had carried away the building mother and father had built. Only one old neighbor remained. The rest had left the inhospitable land for irrigated areas around Billings. As we walked over the barren acres, the nostalgia inspired a flood of emotion and prompted our hearts to worship in gratitude for all the way the Lord had led.

Our family had a big program of welcome home and holiday celebrations scheduled, but in the midst of the gaiety a wire came requesting Leister to report at once to his new job with Bendix in Baltimore, Maryland. Once more Leister had to say goodbye to family and friends and respond to the call of duty.

Since it would likely be the last Christmas for a long time that I could spend with our families, Leister arranged for me to stay for the family festivities. He reported to his first day of work with Bendix at Towson, Maryland, on 10 December 1945.

PERSONNEL RECORD

NAME: Leister Fink Graffis.

DATE OF BIRTH: May 7, 1909. AGE: 36 years.

NATIONALITY: American. RACE: White.

MARITAL STATUS: Married. NO. CHILDREN: None.

WEIGHT: 200 pounds.

EDUCATION

HIGH SCHOOL: American School, Chicago, Ill. (Correspondence school.)

COLLEGE: Three years Elect. Eng. majoring in radio communication at the North Dakota State School of Science, Wahpeton, North Dakota. Two six weeks' summer terms in Trade and Industrial Education at the Colorado State College, Fort Collins, Colorado. Three months' course in electronics at Harvard Univeristy (Navy Pre-radar. Three months' U. H. F. and radar course at M. I. T. (Navy radar engineering).. Six weeks' radio/radar maintenance course at Naval Air Technical Training Command, Corpus Christi, Texas.

EMPLOYMENT RECORD

1923 to 1934: Worked at many different jobs as farm hand and auto and tractor mechanic in small town garages in North Dakota. Completed a four-year high school course by correspondence during this period. Quit to start college in the fall of 1934.

1934 to 1937: Attended college and worked part-time as assistant to the head of the radio department, teaching four classes the third year.

1937 to 1941: Trade School Supervisor and instructor at the State Training School, Mandan, North Dakota. (School of Correction for delinquent boys.) Organized the department, purchased all tools and equipment necessary to establish practical trade courses in machine shop practice, general electricity, including armature winding, radio, house wiring, and auto electrical repair, auto and tractor mechanics, arc and oxy-acetylene welding. One assistant instructor was assigned to this department in 1938. About 175 young men completed the prescribed course of instruction in this department during these four years. In addition to the regular duties of Trade School Supervisor, a National Defense Training Course was conducted by this department as an evening school five nights a week during the winter months of 1940-1941, for the purpose of giving experienced tradesmen refresher courses in machine shop practice and arc and oxy-acetylene welding. Also served as State Advisor for the organization of an N. Y. A. Defense Training Program during this period. Attended Colorado State College during the summers of 1940 and 1941.

1941 to 1942: Precision Assembler for Lockheed Aircraft. Taught machine shop practice part-time in a National Defense Training Course sponsored by Lockheed Aircraft in the Burbank, California, High School.

March 1942 to July 1942: Radio Engineer under Civil Service (P-2 rating) employed by the U. S. Army Signal Corps, Presidio of San Francisco. In charge of all the course of instruction and lesson material used by the state colleges and universities on the west coast engaged in the training of radio and radar technicians for the Signal Corps. Assisted in hiring trainees and instructors and conducted instructor training courses.

August 1942 to October 1942: Inducted into the U. S. Army, assigned to Camp Crowder, Missouri, and put in charge of the F. M. section of the radio maintenance school. Was given an Honorable Discharge to accept a commission in the Naval Reserve as lieutenant junior grade.

November 1942 to September 1943: In training as a radio-radar officer in the Navy Air Corps.

September 1943 to January 1945: Sixteen months' overseas duty in the Pacific as Radio-Radar Officer in charge of all radio, radar, and electrical maintenance and installations on 60 twin engine planes. Personnel assigned to this department numbered over one hundred men.

March 1945 to present date: Radio-Radar Officer in charge of training and the instructional lab for a Naval Radar Training Unit.

Chapter Fourteen
Just a Spot to Call Our Own

When I returned to Leister after spending the holidays with our families, he had found a single room at 205 Allegheny Avenue in Towson, Maryland. While Leister found his place as a staff engineer and assistant to Don Kresge of Bendix Home Radio and TV, I went apartment hunting. After weeks of searching I located a home we inspected together and agreed to purchase. On 16 March 1946, we moved into our own home at 8 Lombardy Place in Towson. The seven-room house was the fulfillment of long-deferred dreams for Leister and me. As we walked under the shade of the sycamore and catalpa trees in our front yard and relaxed under the shade of the weeping willow in our back yard, we dreamed sacred dreams of the future as we anticipated the birth of our first child in December.

Precious are the memories of that Christmas in 1946. Only a year before we had been torn apart while visiting our families in the west. Our togetherness made us ecstatic as we stood by the crib of our first child, Beverly, born December 7. Those were moments too sacred for words, so in worshipful wonder we shared in the mystery and miracle of a new life.

Leister was overwhelmed with a sense of responsibility as he watched over his own little girl. His navy pals knew him as a sound sleeper and joked about it, but Beverly changed all that. He would waken at her faintest cry and rise before I could respond, and he would minister to her night by night. His role as a father was to him a sacred trust.

The demands of his job created a tension with the demands of Leister's heart. He had not anticipated his job as a staff engineer would counter all our dreams of family togetherness. During his first year with Bendix he traveled one hundred thousand miles. He was required to assist and set up displays presenting Bendix home radio and TV to dealers all over the nation. Often a single show would demand two or three weeks away from home.

Back in 1945, when we stopped at the Merchandise Mart on our way west, Leister never thought that in a few years a job with Bendix would bring him back to that same Mart. Leister did not enjoy climbing, but in the line of duty he steeled himself to climb the heights of that same Merchandise Mart—and later the Waldorf-Astoria in New York—to install their first FM antennas.

It was hard to have Leister miss so many of the magic hours of Beverly's beginnings—the first smile, the first word, the first step. Every moment he could spare he spent playing with her, comforting her through the teething tears, kissing her toddler bruises, and training her in bicycle safety as she grew from one phase to the next.

Proudly ours!
Marian and Leister with baby Beverly.
First warm day in 1947.

He brought the first TV in that area to our living room. As Beverly grew and was able to make friends, our living room became a meeting place. Often when Leister came home from work he would find the living room floor decorated wall to wall with children watching "Howdy Doody."

From 1945-1950 Leister served Bendix successively as staff engineer and assistant service manager in the Radio and TV Service Department. In 1949 he transferred to the Technical Publications Department and served as senior technical writer. This was a thing he had been doing ever since the early days at Lockheed, the Signal Corps, and Camp Crowder.

On one occasion when he brought home one of his manuals I was amused. The first directive in the manual told them to plug in the equipment as step number one. I protested, remarking that I considered that an insult to the customer's intelligence. He did not and responded by saying that their serviceman had been called out on complaints that their equipment simply would not work. When the serviceman got there he found the only problem was that the equipment had not been plugged in.

Chapter Fifteen
New Heights, New Sites

One thing in our life remained constant—our spiritual priorities. We attended the Calvary Baptist Church of Towson and were not content to be spectators. Leister served as Sunday School superintendent, teacher, chairman of the deacon board, and as a Scout leader. He was to continue scouting for many years until he was awarded the Silver Beaver, the highest leadership award given to volunteer Scout leaders.

I was busy as a mother, Girl Scout leader, and teacher of adult classes in tailoring. My Girl Scout leaders loved having our little girl in their meetings. This, however, exposed her to childhood diseases. Leister's mother had been proud that her twin boys escaped the childhood sicknesses. Leister gave Beverly every attention while she had them. The measles and chicken pox he escaped as a child caught up with him, and he suffered through both of them himself. The brightest spot of the week for Leister was the babysitting job he had with Beverly all to himself while I taught my evening classes in tailoring.

Meanwhile things were happening which were to infringe on our family times. Late in the summer of 1950 Colonel George Getz of the United States Air Force asked to meet with the general manager of Bendix Radio, E. K. Foster. The air force was purchasing Bendix-built long-range radar sets known as FPS-3. When they were installed, the air force had no one trained with the "know-how" or logistics to maintain and operate them. Bendix did not want to assume this responsibility, for they felt it would distract them from their production goals.

The air force would not take "No" for an answer. They arranged another meeting, this time bringing to the Bendix plant at Towson the highest level of air force command. Bendix decided to accept the challenge. When they thought of a man to head this new department, the logical person was the man who was writing the instruction manual. W. L. Webb sent out an interdepartmental bulletin.

INTERDEPARTMENTAL

BENDIX RADIO

October 16, 1950

To: All Department Heads

From: Mr. W. L. Webb

        Effective today, Mr. Leister F. Graffis is appointed Chief
Field Engineer in charge of field engineering service, technical
representatives, and maintenance training programs.

        Many new Government projects are being undertaken which will
soon require that Bendix Radio provide extensive field engineering
services.

        Mr. Graffis is at present heavily engaged in the instruction
book program for FPS-3 equipment. The urgent need for these books
makes it necessary for Mr. Graffis to continue to devote part of
his time to their preparation and he will therefore commence his
field engineering program on a part time basis.

        Mr. Graffis will report to H. W. Giesecke in his new assign-
ment and, at the start, will devote Monday of each week to the field
engineering work. The telephone extension for the field engineering
office is 494.

        Your cooperation with Mr. Graffis will be greatly appreciated
In particular, Mr. Graffis will be happy to have your assistance in
locating qualified applicants for employment as field engineers.

                                           W. L. Webb

WLW:mh

After Mr. Webb issued the 16 October 1950 bulletin, Leister went through hectic days of transition. Four days of the week he concentrated on the FPS-3 manuals. The first of these were due off the assembly line December 1. The radar set was to be installed at the Eniwetok Atoll in the Marshall Islands to control aircraft for an atomic test scheduled for early in 1951.

Meanwhile, news of the new Field Engineering Department was hitting the headlines.

Graffis Named To Bendix Post

Leister F. Graffis has been appointed chief field engineer of the Bendix Radio Division of Bendix Aviation Corporation in Towson.

The announcement was made by F. L. Webb, director of research and engineering, who said Graffis will be in charge of field engineering service, maintenance training programs and technical representatives assisting Government agencies in installation and maintenance.

Work Overseas

Members of Mr. Graffis's department will furnish technical assistance in radar, communication and navigation equipment. They will work throughout the United States and at some overseas points.

Mr. Graffis was formerly associated with the Technical Publications Department and served as assistant service manager of the Television and Broadcast Receiver Sales Department.

As a lieutenant commander in the Navy during the last war, Mr. Graffis helped set up search radar equipment on the West Coast and supervised preparation of instructional material for all radio technician schools in that area.

Graffis Heads Field Group

Leister. F. Graffis, of Technical Publications, has been appointed Chief Field Engineer, according to an announcement by W. L. Webb.

In his new capacity, Graffis will be in charge of field engineering service, maintenance training programs, and will direct the activities of technical represatatives of the Division who will assist government agencies in installation and maintenance.

Les currently is sharing his time in winding up his work on the preparation of technical literature and in setting up an organization to carry on the extensive field services. Ultimately, personnel of his group will be assigned to work in many parts of the country, as well as to places outside the borders.

It will be the responsibility of this group, operating as Department 70, to furnish technical assistance to customers in installing and maintaining radar, communication, and navigation equipment.

Prior to his association with Technical Publications, Graffis was Assistant Service Manager of the Television and Broadcast Receiver Sales Department.

He was a Lieutenant Commander in the Navy before coming to Bendix. During his Service stay, Les was engaged in the set up of search radar equipment on the west coast, supervised the preparation of instructional material for all radio technician schools in that area, completed radar courses at Harvard and MIT; and served two years overseas in maintenance and installation of electronic equipment in land based bombers.

His civilian employment before the war included five years teaching experience in trade schools. Graffis was one of the directors of the North Dakota State N.Y.A. training program, and was instrumental in the establishment of the teacher training courses for shop instructors in the national defense program of the same state.

The first duty of the new Department of Field Engineering was to train men to operate and maintain the long-range radar equipment coming off the Bendix assembly lines. To do this a school was needed. The birth of this new school was to be celebrated with a grandiose dedication ceremony on Armed Forces Day in 1951. Leister gave only token enthusiasm to the elaborate plans, for at about the same time Mr. Webb announced the birth of a new department, our doctor had made a very private announcement that Leister and I were to expect the birth of our second child in early June. With our little girl Elaine, born June 21, resting peacefully, I was to read about the dedication day as reported in the *P.R.S.M.A. News*.

AIR FORCE MEN TO BE TRAINED AT BENDIX UNIT
BENDIX SCHOOL FOR ELECTRONICS DEDICATED IN ARMED FORCES DAY CEREMONIES

An industry-sponsored school to train Air Force personnel in the maintenance of military electronics equipment was dedicated here today in connection with observance of Armed Forces Day.

Located at Pimlico Airport, where it occupies a 40-acre tract including two hangars, the Bendix School for Electronics was officially opened in ceremonies attended by U.S.A.F. officials and executives of the Bendix Radio Division of Bendix Aviation Corporation, sponsors of the new training unit.

Col. Robert Griffin, director of communications and electronics at Langley Air Force Base, Langley, Virginia, was principal speaker at the dedication ceremonies, which also featured a demonstration of radar equipment.

Other speakers included, Edward K. Foster, Bendix vice president and general manager of the Radio Division; and Lt. Col. J. Walton Colvin, of the Maryland Wing, Civil Air Patrol.

Both Air Force personnel and Bendix field engineers will be instructed at the new school in the maintenance of the highly complex electronic equipment, including radar and navigation devices, essential in operating today's military aircraft. With an enrollment made up largely of Air Force men, the school is operating two "shifts" daily with a faculty of 10 Bendix and two U.S.A.F. instructors. Additional courses now planned will double the activity in the near future. For Air Force personnel, the school's eight-week course represents the final phase of training in electronic equipment.

W. T. Spicer, chief engineer of Field Service Departments for Bendix Radio, and Leister Graffis, chief field engineer, are supervising the electronics school, which is expected soon to enroll students from all branches of the armed forces.

A pioneer in the development and manufacture of radar, aircraft radio and many other types of precision communication equipment, Bendix Radio Division is now shipping $1,000,000 worth of electronics equipment weekly to the armed forces and has $30,000,000 in defense work subcontracted to smaller firms or in the process of negotiation.

The division recently added 50,000 square feet of floor space to its plant in nearby Towson to facilitate production of military orders and has constructed a large unit for the testing and erection of heavy radar equipment. All of the Navy's wartime and peacetime GCA radar was manufactured at the Towson plant.

In addition to training Air Force and other service personnel, the Bendix School for Electronics is training a large group of electronics specialists who will be sent out with Air Force and Navy operational units to provide a professional grade of assistance in the operation and maintenance of radar equipment. Some have already gone to overseas locations and eight additional field engineers departed for unannounced destinations last week. Bendix expects to have over 100 trained field engineers assigned to the Air Force by the end of this year.

Our baby Elaine on the day of her dedication, wearing the dress Leister wore at his dedication. The dress was entirely handmade by a great aunt.

The new School for Electronics was located at Pimlico, Maryland. It was housed in an old airport. The maintenance crew had to evict the birds that had resided there unchallenged for years as they moved in and out of the three thousand broken windows. Classrooms were prepared and Department Seventy was growing into an efficient school—even if sometimes they had to lay planks to keep from walking in water.

In his new role as chief engineer and director of the Bendix School of Electronics, Leister was to have a clerk-typist. As he interviewed applicants, he was biased toward a mature secretary. There was to be a constant flow of about twenty-five young air force men passing through the school every two months, and he felt an attractive young secretary would be a distraction.

When Britannia Siltman came for an interview, he sensed she was the secretary he needed. Bendix offered another position but she accepted the offer of Field Engineering. During the two decades she worked with Leister, he knew that the Lord had given her to his department. She became Leister's veritable "Girl Friday." She understood the department and Leister's thinking so well she could pre-write much of his correspondence, and he would have to do very little editing.

When much of the department's material became highly classified, she was a constant watchdog, guarding lest they might be charged with releasing classified material to unauthorized people.

"Brit," as everyone called her, was truly indispensable. She would even stay after hours to do secretarial work for Leister's church or scouting activities.

To the constant flow of men that came and went from the school, Brit was a mother figure, counselor, confidant, and button sewer. In the early days as a telephone switchboard operator she was a rapport builder for the whole department.

To most Baltimorians, the name "Pimlico" calls forth visions of thundering hooves, roaring crowds and torn-up daily double tickets. But to Bill Spicer and Les Graffis, "Pimlico" has been nothing but hard steady work. In a few short months, these two men have done much to make Dept. 70 (Field Engineering and Bendix School for Electronics) a reality.

Already the school, located at old Pimlico Airport on Smith Avenue, is turning out 32 highly skilled Radar Maintenance Men a month. The majority of these men are Air Force personnel with a sprinkling of Bendix civilians also taking the course. All are receiving specialized instruction in Bendix built equipment.

The students of the five classes now in session are young, clean cut boys in their early twenties. For the most part, they come from small towns scattered across the country. The boys are from Mississippi, Washington, New England, Michigan and Maryland. They work hard over textbooks, equipment and schematic drawings for eight weeks and then return to their posts in the field. Bendix is not the only manufacturer with a similiar school in operation. By the end of the summer nearly every maker of government electronic gear will have schools open for students.

The next time a fellow worker tells you that he is going to Pimlico, it might be well to ask for details before you give him two dollars to bet on Uncle Milty in the fourth.

Page 13

53

Chapter Sixteen
Keeping in Touch

Mr. L. F. Graffis, May Spotlight Speaker

BEHIND THE SPOTLIGHT

Mr. Leister (Les) Graffis, Chief Field Engineer and Director of the Bendix School of Electronics, will put the spotlight on "Field Engineering" at the May meeting. "Les" came to Bendix in 1945 as a radio engineer. He served successively as Staff Engineer, Assistant to the Service Manager, and Assistant Service Manager in the Radio and TV Service Department. Later, he spent a year as a Senior Technical Writer in with the Technical Publications Department. In January 1951, he was made Chief Field Engineer and organized the Field Engineering Department. This department is responsible for providing factory maintenance for the military and CAA Bendix built equipment in use around the world. It also conducts a training course for Bendix field engineers as well as customer personnel.

Mr. Graffis has attended Colorado State College, Harvard University, and M.I.T. He is a senior member of the I.R.E. and is at present serving on the R.E.T.M.A. Electronic Operation and Maintenance subcommittee. He is listed in Who's Who in America, as well as Who's Who in Engineering.

In a 8 July 1954 newsletter to his employees, Leister reported that two management clubs had been organized in which Department Seventy was taking an active interest.

The YMCA in Towson sponsored an Industrial Management Club. In 1954 Leister was on their board of directors. The second was the Bendix Management Club, which was an inter-plant organization composed of all the salaried employees of Bendix Radio.

In the newsletter, Leister wrote, "It may appear that there is an overlapping in objectives between the two organizations, but after attending two or three meetings of each, I have decided that there is a definite need for both. In one we rub elbows with men of other companies and learn of their problems. In the Bendix Club we become better acquainted with people within our own company."

In May of 1955, Leister was the Spotlight Speaker at a dinner meeting held in the American Legion Hall at Towson.

In his speech at that May meeting Leister stressed that there must exist a mutual trust between the field engineer and his home base. Leister never brought shop home and always tried to shelter us from stresses he faced. From the sidelines I concluded that if the number of gifts he received in the early years was criterion for the level of trust attained, he certainly must have succeeded in building that mutual trust with his worldwide family.

One example of such gifts was an elaborate barometer, hygrometer, and thermometer delivered to him for his birthday from Germany. By December he had finally convinced his widely scattered family that he was sincere in his conviction that it was not ethical for him to exploit his position by accepting their gifts. Then we were flooded with Christmas cards. There were hand-painted cards of silk, cards in many languages, and in many exotic designs. He told his men they would be among his souvenirs. I attempted to post them until our living room was papered wall to wall with greetings.

SPOTLIGHT ON FIELD ENGINEERING

 At the May meeting, Mr. L. F. Graffis, Chief Field Engineer and Director of the Bendix School of Electronics, placed the Field Engineering Department in the spotlight.

The mission of the field engineer, Mr. Graffis pointed out, is to keep the customer satisfied and to keep the company informed of field conditions and problems. The technical end of the Field Engineer's task is not ordinarily too difficult on well built equipment; ninety per cent of the job is in exercising the art of diplomacy--"satisfying the customer". Mr. Graffis added that any illusion of "romanticism" associated with Field Engineering can be quickly dispelled by an assignment in Thule or Alaska. Rather, it is a 24-hour-per-day job that requires special attributes not nearly so necessary in most other vocations.

Prospective Field Engineers are given a personality index test as well as the standard battery of general and technical knowledge tests. Before a man is sent into the field, he must complete eight weeks of intensive technical training on the specific type of equipment he will maintain. This is followed by additional training either in the depot or with one of the mobile labs, where he is under the guidance of more experienced personnel.

Mr. Graffis stressed the fact that there exists a mutual trust between the Field Engineer and the department. An engineer is never criticized before his side of the story is known and is continually reminded that he has not been forgotten. Each man is completely on his own, and, as a Bendix representative, he must remember that Bendix is judged by his conduct both on and off the job. To fulfill his responsibilities he must "display good horse sense and at times have the wisdom of Solomon", since supervision is difficult due to the distant location of many of the sites.

Mr. Graffis was very optimistic as to the future of Field Engineering. He pointed out that with the development of increasingly complex equipment, the need is growing for Contractor Maintenance Support, that this service cannot be a gift, and that dollar for dollar Bendix Field Engineering has more to offer in the way of service than other companies. Mr. Graffis emphasized that Field Engineering presently has some 300 engineers in the field and is continuing to expand. Field Engineering is here to stay.

Leister was growing in world consciousness as he felt a very personal responsibility for his growing family of engineers. We at home could only sense part of the pressure. The children and I were compelled to hold their father loosely, for he was now in the Orient, now in frigid Iceland, now in torrid Africa, now in destinations unrevealed for security reasons.

When he was able to sit down with us at the dinner table he would be an attentive father giving an undistracted ear as the children shared with him the joys, achievements, and concerns of their child world. Often the dinner table was Leister's only touch with his two darlings, Beverly and Elaine.

Beverly and Elaine Graffis

We had to have a large date calendar, both on our wall and on Brit's desk to keep track of his community, civic, and church appointments.

As chief field engineer Leister had great empathy for the engineers stationed in remote areas. It was important to support the morale of these men in far-out places. The location of some of these stations was sometimes highly secret.

The Field Engineering Story

"Watch your step, the catwalk is icy," says a young man at a radar site in northern Alaska. Somewhere on the Atlantic seaboard another young fellow looks up at a radar antenna that groans against 80-mile headwinds. And in Frankfurt, Germany, another man is patiently explaining a complex mechanism to a fatigue-clad G. I. All three are doing the same job. They're Bendix field engineers.

Young and Virile

Field Engineering is the thriving young-ster of the Bendix family. Three years old last April, it has already grown to global size. You can find Bendix men in England, Iceland, Germany, Spain, North Africa, Newfoundland, Korea, Alaska, any of the Islands of Japan, and, of course, these United States. If you study the locations of our radar sites on a globe, you'll discover that they describe an irregular arc around Communist Russia. A site usually in-cludes about 250 Air Force people and one Bendix field engineer.

Engineers' Responsibility

"Our first responsibility is to help the Air Force give the folks at home time to find shelter, avert panic and to get the fighters into the sky if the Red bombers ever come," observes a field engineer whose job takes him within sight of the Siberian border. The radar

Page 4

L. F. Graffis, Chief Field Engineer

network, he says, must furnish "those few all-important minutes of warning." That, in a nutshell, is the job that Field Engineering is helping to do.

A lot of work and planning go into the job. What happens, for instance, when a vital part of a set wears out in an operation somewhere north of every-place right in the middle of nowhere? You have to have a system set up to deal with such emergencies. There was,

Bendix Beam, November 1954

for example, the case of the radar antenna on Okinawa. It was blown away in a heavy tornado. That station was operating again in "jig" time.

Delivering the goods is not the only responsibility of Field Engineering. "The job is 50 per cent service and 50 per cent tact and diplomacy," was the way an engineer stationed in England

Ralph Martino, Field Engineer, adjusts ASR-3 PPI in Knoxville tower.

put it. A field engineer is also a salesman of a sort, a globetrotter, a pioneer, and must, as a matter of course, know his product as well as he knows his

Page 5

name. He must have the ingenuity and initiative to work entirely on his own.

Air Force Impetus

The Air Force in 1950, discussed with Bendix Radio the possibility of obtaining the manufacturer's assistance in installation and maintenance of complex radar equipment. Out of these discussions came the Field Engineering Program.

Walt Becker, Field Engineer, at far western radar sight.

Bendix Beam, November 1954

Since the inception of the Department of Field Engineering on 19 October 1950, the engineers had to have security clearance. If there appeared in an engineer's application anything that the National Defense Department might question, he would not be accepted by the Bendix School for Electronics. Brit had secret clearance and Leister, top secret.

In Leister's office there was a constant tension lest highly classified materials should be released to unauthorized persons. It was not uncommon for government secret agents to drop by the office with phony credentials to check their alertness. Brit's vigilance kept them above rebuke.

Chapter Seventeen
Extending Our Sites

Early in the fifties, Leister would tell me he was sure the phenomenal growth of Field Engineering would soon level off. Again and again he would come home and report to the contrary. Orders and contracts kept pouring in. In those early days, he said if Field Engineering ever grew to five hundred employees, it would be unmanageable. By October of 1956, they had reached 534 employees and were sending out supervisors with two full-time recruiters to find engineers willing to train for the remote radar sites around the world.

Up until 1957, Bendix Field Engineering might have been defined as a company supporting and servicing heavy ground radar equipment guarding the security of our nation. On Leister's passport application, his reason for travel was listed as "Supervision and liaison–re United States contracts" for the armed services.

The year 1958 was being designated International Geophysical year (IGY-58). Magazines and media were discussing all sorts of goals and agendas. Leister and I listened with interest and he read avidly about projections being made on every hand. We never envisioned all the tensions that were to converge to further influence our family life style.

Chief Scientist Charles McMullen of Bendix Radio attended a briefing of the Naval Research Laboratory to discuss the procurement of a package to track satellites. The United States planned to celebrate the year by putting into orbit a grapefruit-sized satellite. RCA had the contract to build the satellite, and Bendix had a contract to prepare portable satellite tracking systems housed in trailers and called MINITRACK. Since Field Engineering was assigned part of the Bendix contract, Leister was busy getting this whole new system on track.

Dr. Wernher Von Braun, a German scientist, had been in charge of rocketry for the Germans. When he saw the advance of the Red Army, he and his colleagues surrendered to the United States forces in Bavaria. Dr. Von Braun and 118 of his colleagues were hired by the United States and sent to Fort Bliss, Texas, to refine the V-2 rocket for our use. By 1957, he had been moved to Huntsville, Alabama, to Redstone's Space Flight Center, and was working on the grapefruit-sized satellite, Vanguard, which the United States planned to launch.

What shocks were ahead! The United States watched with dismay as in October 1957, Russia orbited a satellite around the earth. In close succession, they launched Sputnik I and II. Sensing we were taking a back seat and becoming second rate to Russia in space, the nation, Bendix, and Leister began serious introspection. It was a great blow to our national self-image and pride.

While Russia was making one advanced step forward after another, the United States' space effort went into a tailspin. The attempt to launch the Vanguard was aborted when it exploded on the launch pad. The success of Russia's space program brought fears to the American mind. A sense of insecurity intensified as we realized that Russia now had the capacity to spy on us, and a feeling of defenselessness invaded all minds.

In the midst of the national frenzy, Leister's home front was in a state of flux. The military had complained that the Field Engineering facility, where the Bendix School for Electronics was housed, was not up to their standard for housing their trainees; aside from that, Field Engineering had quite outgrown the facility. The latter half of 1958 was one of intense preoccupation for Leister. The children and I were on his heart, but the world seemed to be on his shoulders while the total facility was moved from Pimlico to Owings Mills.

In 1959 tensions continued to mount. Russia was sending up one spacecraft after another and was making great strides. They had sent a live dog into space. January saw them launch Luna I, which achieved earth-escape velocity. Their Luna II impacted the moon and their Luna III took pictures of the far side of the moon. Russia's successes only deepened our humiliation and aggravated our pressures. Nikita Kruschev jeered about American "oranges" in space. Three spacecraft the United States had launched had a combined weight of sixty-five pounds, while a Russian Sputnik carried 2,129 pounds of instruments, and circled over most of the earth's inhabited area.

The humiliation served to "galvanize the United States into action."[1] There was no relief in sight. Russia announced that they were preparing to put a man in space. Our government was tense in the knowledge that the Soviets now had the ability to orbit a satellite over the United States and spy on us. Washington proposed a MINITRACK system to keep an eye on satellites. NASA asked Murray Weingarten, assistant to Leister, how soon Bendix could get a tracking system into operation. He responded with, "How about 50 percent manning in thirty days and 100 percent in one hundred days?" NASA awarded the contract to Bendix, and Field Engineering had the tracking system fully manned in forty-five days. When Bendix Field Engineering so successfully answered the challenge, they were chosen to maintain all the tracking sites.[2]

Leister tried to protect the children and me from the fears that were shaking the nation, but there seemed to be no end to the pressures that were converging on him. To counter the Soviet goal of putting a man into space, the United States proposed a Mercury program. Dr. Werner Von Braun was directed to proceed with project Mercury.

Before MINITRACK, Bendix Field Engineering was working only with highly classified information of the United States military. When they were awarded the contract with MINITRACK, they also became a civilian operation, and their sites were to outdo "the cow that jumped over the moon." They were in the field of space science, and their goal was to track all spacecraft. Radar sites operated primarily for national defense. Supervising and administering these two distinct programs actually kept Leister "up in the air." About this time, the airlines sent a certificate congratulating Leister on having completed a million miles of air travel. After we had a good look at it, Leister had it framed and hung in his brand new office at Owings Mills.

In the early days of the Korean War, Leister went on a mission to Japan for Bendix Field Engineering. He visited their far eastern headquarters at Tokyo with Jim Young, the Bendix local supervisor. Jim had been a radio operator on a P.T. boat in the Pacific. At the time of Leister's visit, Jim had a secretary whose father lost his life when his boat sank during World War II. On checking records, Jim discovered that his own P.T. boat had targeted a boat in that area on the date her father lost his life.

On that same mission, Leister visited the radar site at Hokkaido, Japan. This was the same site to which Leister had flown on bombing missions during World War II, while he was stationed on Attu in the Aleutian Islands.

In front of the Tokyo Precision Instrument Company (Bendix Japanese depot and licensee) are Frank O'Doherty, then of Department 81, Mr. Hashi, President of the company, Jim Young, Les Graffis, Mr. Faruki, Director of the company, and Chuck Hartwigson. You can read "Bendix" in Japanese on the far right.

Local labor at a radar site in Japan.

The coming of a radar site creates a stir in this remote settlement in northern Hokkaido. Most of these people have never seen a white man.

Chapter Eighteen
None Indispensable

On the morning of 4 March 1960, as Leister left for work, he reminded me that since he had an evening meeting in Washington, he would not be home for dinner. During that morning his secretary, Brit, kept prodding about his need for a haircut. At his noon break, he decided to take her advice and take time out for the recommended haircut.

Shortly after he left the office, two telephone men assigned to the plant to care for their mushrooming network of phones stopped by Leister's office. They told Brit they had just come off the road and saw a wrecked black VW they were sure belonged to Mr. Graffis. Brit said it couldn't have been he, for he had only left a short time ago. They insisted, however, and said the ambulance had just driven away when they passed the scene.

Brit decided she had better check, so she called the hospital. They said that they did have a Mr. Graffis in emergency and that he wouldn't tell them if he had insurance. When Brit told me the story later, she said she really "blew her top." She asked them what they expected from a man in trauma. She said she told them that the man was the president of Field Engineering for Bendix and had all the insurance any man in this world needed. She told them she was going to dispatch two executives to the hospital immediately.

What a shock to me when the telephone rang and a professional voice asked if this was the home of Leister Graffis. Next they told me he was in emergency care in the Sinai Hospital as the result of an automobile accident.

I rushed out to the trusty Buick and hurried down to the hospital. I was really disturbed, and let them know it, when they would not let me in the room and said two men were in the room with him. When they finally admitted me, I found Colonel Swoger and Vic Eckman in the room. These were the two men Brit had sent from Bendix to guarantee Leister would get every care. My first impression as he lay there on the hospital bed was not as devastating as the truth that was to surface later. When we saw the car we marveled that anyone could have gotten out of it alive.

What actually happened was that a car coming from the opposite direction on Reisterstown Road went out of control on the icy highway. It then slid into Leister's VW and crushed him under a big tractor trailer.

The real extent of Leister's injuries was not discovered in the emergency examination given to him. The doctor who made the full examination told him later that his first prognosis when all tests were in was that Leister would be confined to bed for a year. He did not tell Bendix that, and they gave him a month's leave of absence.

In the weeks that followed Leister went through a nightmare of agony from his multiple injuries. He had to live in an aluminum strait jacket and wear a neck collar. By this time he had two assistants, Murray Weingarten and Irwin Sieron, who carried on in his absence. They would give memos to Leister's secretary, and each evening Brit would stop at the house and go over the memos with Leister then return his opinions and decisions to the men the next day.

What would have broken many men only revealed the mettle of my husband. It was heart-breaking to stand by and see him suffer physical pain and the emotional trauma of being sidelined. Brit's daily visits were a most significant help to his morale—second only to his confidence in the faithfulness of God. Her consulting him helped alleviate the mental anguish that was inherent in a man of his stamina. He never had any handicap sideline him before, but this was something he could not shake off.

Bendix RADIO

FIELD ENGINEERING REPORTER

VOL. II   MARCH 1960   NO. 3

 ## HEADQUARTERS NEWS ITEMS

On March 4, 1960, Mr. Les Graffis was involved in a rather unfortunate automobile accident at the intersection of Reisterstown Road and Mount Wilson Lane, Baltimore, Maryland. His injuries included a cracked rib, compressed vertebra, concussion, cuts and bruises.

Mr. Joseph Hunt, a Pikesville telephone installer, was the first person at Mr. Graffis' side after the accident and he immediately applied first aid. This on-the-spot first aid may have contributed considerably to Mr. Graffis' remarkable recovery.

As of Sunday, March 27, 1960, Les has recovered sufficiently to sit up and his constant dizzy sensation has been reduced to a minimum. Naturally the compressed vertebra has been quite troublesome and will require a few more additional weeks to mend.

FROM THE MANAGER'S DESK

Many of you won't know until you have received this Reporter that I had the misfortune of being involved in an automobile accident on March 4th. Suffice to say I required hospitalization (Sinai Hospital) but am presently recuperating at home and will remain there for three or four more weeks. Although a compressed vertebra is not very serious, it does require some time to heal. I mention my accident not to dwell upon the gory details of what happened to myself or my Volkswagon, but instead to talk about that indispensable person.

During the past few weeks in bed I have, quite naturally, had more time to think about such subjects as the indispensable person, than I would have had while in the office. Certainly this is a most inappropriate time for me to be absent from the office by my own standards at least. Normally, I would have said it was impossible for me to take time off with so many proposals in the Department and all the new contracts coming up for negotiation.

But in spite of all my ideas about being indispensable at this time, I find that things simply do go on without me. I recall reading an article on a similar subject sometime ago, in which the example was given that if a person wanted to realize how much of a vacuum he would leave, place his hand in a pail of water and observe the hole which is left when it is removed. Maybe it takes something like this to convince any one of us that the world will go along pretty much the same whether we are in there pitching or not.

I want to thank so many of you for remembering me with telegrams, get well cards and of course, personal visits from those who were in a position to call. I sincerely appreciate all your kindnesses much more than mere words can possibly express.

Here's hoping that next month I'm back in that indispensable spot.

FROM THE MANAGER'S DESK

Nobody could have told me when I dictated last month's message that I would be again dictating this months from home. The truth is that the doctor hasn't been as considerate as I expected or maybe I should say I was probably worse off than I thought. I am still at home in a back brace and "horsecollar" that holds my head in a straight-up position. Not meaning to complain, for I'm very thankful to even be alive and talking about it, I can assure all of you it would be quite difficult to devise a more uncomfortable way to live than to be in a back brace and collar for twenty-four hours a day. Even though I have been very impatient and somewhat amazed that I haven't been able to get back to work before this, my doctor and the specialists all claim amazement at my speedy recovery. I have always believed in listening to the experts, therefore I must believe they are correct and I was in error in thinking I could be back in the office within two or three weeks after the March 4th accident.

Again I wish to repeat, even more enthusiastically and emphatically, my thanks and appreciation for all the letters, cards and those who stopped by to see me during these very long and tedious days and weeks. A person who has never been confined, including myself, has no idea how much such things are truly appreciated until you find yourself restricted either to a hospital or home and are unable to do many of the normal everyday activities.

I want to publicly thank all the supervisors who have carried on the work of our Field Engineering Department so efficiently during my absence. I'm confident I haven't been informed of all the difficulties encountered, but I am confident they have been carrying on most capably, in spite of these problems; for this I thank each and every one of you. Maybe I shouldn't predict being back at the office when this is due next month, but I sure have every hope of being there!

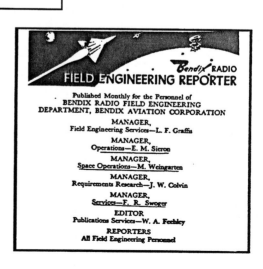

Bendix RADIO
FIELD ENGINEERING REPORTER

Published Monthly for the Personnel of
BENDIX RADIO FIELD ENGINEERING
DEPARTMENT, BENDIX AVIATION CORPORATION

MANAGER,
Field Engineering Services—L. F. Graffis

MANAGER,
Operations—E. M. Sieron

MANAGER,
Space Operations—M. Weingarten

MANAGER,
Requirements Research—J. W. Colvin

MANAGER,
Services—F. R. Swoger

EDITOR
Publications Services—W. A. Fechley

REPORTERS
All Field Engineering Personnel

Chapter Nineteen
"Up in the Air I Go Flying Again"

Leister had just gone out on a Sunday afternoon call 23 July 1961, when a call came ordering him to prepare for an emergency flight to Greenland at once. He had not done any out-of-the-country flying since his accident. I immediately tried to track him down. When he arrived at the house he learned he was to be ready to fly to Thule, Greenland, in a few hours. An order had come from General Chidlaw, a four-star general, and commander of the U.S. Air Defense Command at Colorado Springs, which demanded immediate attention.

Landing in Greenland, there was a top-level conference at Thule with staff and administrators, and then a group of them flew four hundred miles to a tracking station located in a radome on the ice cap. The radomes are built on a platform suspended on jacks that keep them elevated forty feet above the snow level. These jacks permit them to be lifted as the snow level rises and also permits the snow to blow through beneath them instead of piling up and submerging them.

The staff at the radome truly were happy with any touch from the outside. However, the supposed emergency turned out only to vindicate the procedure that had been carried out there. The general had complained because while visiting there he had no direct line of communication to his headquarters in Colorado. When the full problem was reviewed, Bendix and all firms involved were found to have serviced the site in full accord with military specifications. Those remote sites, for security reasons, were to have exactly the pattern of communication systems that had been installed. In reality there was no emergency.

MORE ABOUT ICEBOXES—
Greenland and Iceland

More frigid duty is available to the Bendix field engineer in Greenland and Iceland. Pictures are few and information slight about these two radar defense areas because of security restrictions.

Most publicized base in the area is at Thule (pronounced to rhyme with coolie). That site was super-secret until a national magazine publicized it in a widely distributed article recently.

Living conditions for our field engineers in these areas closely parallel those in Alaska.

This bleak landscape in Iceland is dominated by the huge Bendix radome which houses Bendix-built radar equipment. It gets so cold in these parts that auto and truck motors have to be kept running constantly. Even food freezers have to be heated in this Arctic wilderness.

Thule, Greenland.
On a 10,000 feet of ice, which rises four feet a year, the radome
is an a platform equipped with jacks to keep it forty feet above ice.
Leister Graffis is on the right.

A PBY patrol plane equipped with skis typical of aircraft
in which Leister flew in the Aleutians.

Chapter Twenty
"Up In the Air and Down"

As early as 1958 Leister started writing a series of letters to the corporate management of Bendix presenting the need for group status for Field Engineering. He felt his division had outgrown the status of a dependent of Bendix Radio. Elements of the tax structure and management procedure made reporting back to Bendix Radio as a subordinate awkward and costly in time and efficiency.

Leister's letters led to intensified discussion. Months of complicated dialogue kept it pending. Finally on 1 January 1962, Bendix Field Engineering Corporation started operating as a wholly owned subsidiary of Bendix Corporation with BFEC as its acronym.

Since the birth of NASA, the space program became a civilian rather than a military operation. Some of the work was opened to industrial contractors, and leading entrepreneurs competed for bids advertised by NASA.

To present a bid required months of work and research. When four contracts on which BFEC had bid were lost to competitors, Leister decided to aim high and bid for the launch support services at the John F. Kennedy Space Center.

BFEC came up with a winning proposal in competition with such aerospace giants as Boeing, Chrysler, Douglas, Convair, and Westinghouse. This reinforced BFEC's image as a strong partner of NASA. BFEC was truly flying high![1]

Seated: L.F. Graffis (Bendix) and M. E. Haworth, Jr. (Deputy Chief, Procurement
Division, GH) signing Merritt Island Launch Support contract, NASA Kennedy
Space Center, 2 October 1964. Standing left to right: Frank Vaughn, Director (Bendix);
Byron C. Driskill, Jr., GH63 Contracting Officer and Contracting Officer's Representative
(NASA); and Worth Meigs, Manager, Business Management (Bendix) looking on.

THE JOHN F. KENNEDY SPACE CENTER PROGRAM

Lift-off of the Gemini IV spacecraft on June 3, 1965.

Bendix Field Engineering was awarded a three-year $17 million (estimated total) NASA contract for launch support services at the John F. Kennedy Space Center during the latter part of 1964.

Bendix provides the Kennedy Center launch services in the following areas: operation of Launch complex 39 (the center of launch activities for the Apollo program), Saturn V engineering support services, technical shop operations, propellant services, ordnance storage and checkout, materials testing and cleaning services, and converter-compressor facility operations. Presently there are approximately 700 Bendix employees there and this total is expected to increase to 1000 by the end of this calendar year.

The following pictures display some of the Bendix activities at the Space Center.

Bendix technicians at the control console of the Tenney vacuum chamber, which is used to evaluate new systems under simulated high altitude conditions. Post flight checks on Gemini hardware are also conducted in this chamber.

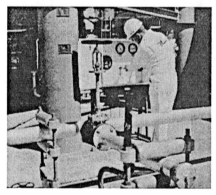

A Bendix technician checks the liquid level indicators on the 35,000 gallon liquid nitrogen storage tank at the launch complex 34/37 converter compressor facility.

TRUST THYSELF.

AIR FORCE SYSTEMS COMMAND ZERO DEFECTS PARTICIPATION AWARD

Captain R. P. Dawson (right), USN, Chief of Defense Contract Administration Services, Baltimore District, presented the Air Force Systems Command's Zero Defects Participation Award to Mr. L. F. Graffis, President of Bendix Field Engineering Corporation, on February 18, 1966. This award is most likely the first given to a field service organization, and the first AFSC Zero Defects Award presented within The Bendix Corporation.

Also representing DCAS were Major Barnes, G. R. Allison, and L. M. Dooley. The DCAS representatives were accompanied to Field Engineering Headquarters by Mr. Glenn Randolph of Bendix Radio. Other Bendix Field Engineering personnel on hand for the presentation were: Murray Weingarten, Vice-President; C. L. Greenslit, Vice-President; and A. S. Moberly, Quality Assurance Manager and coordinator of the company's Zero Defects Program.

The following is a quote from Colonel W. S. Collinson, Director of DCAS, Philadelphia, to L. F. Graffis, President of BFEC:

"We of the Philadelphia Regional Office take justifiable pride in presenting this award from the Air Force Systems Command for not only does it affirm our nomination of your organization for recognition in the Air Force Industrial Zero Defects Program, but it further serves as "proof positive" of your contribution to the overall national effort, which in turn reflects most favorably upon DCASR–Philadelphia."

A congratulatory telegram was received from the top Bendix Corporation executives, Mr. A. P. Fontaine and Mr. George Stoll, regarding this award.

When May Graffis helped her twin boys swing on their rope swing under the cottonwood tree as she recited Robert Louis Stevenson's song, she never dreamed that the poem was almost prophetic of one of her good swingers.

"Up in the air I go flying again,
Up in the air and down."

By January 1967 NASA had launched a sequence of twelve Gemini space craft. BFEC was busy operating and maintaining the launch support facilities for these launchings. This kept Leister commuting between BFEC and the Kennedy Space Center. Things were moving full speed ahead toward the launching of Apollo I. Already ground testings were in process. On January 27, Leister and I were invited to a NASA banquet in Washington, D.C. It was a festive celebration with a great air of confidence and a growing sense of progress toward our goal of catching up with Russia's marathon space achievements.

In the midst of the banquet, a voice broke into the festivities announcing that a fire had erupted in Apollo I during a routine ground test, and Gus Grissom, Edward White, and Roger Chaffee were dead from carbon monoxide asphyxiation. What a change of mood came over the banqueters. It all happened three weeks before a scheduled flight. The test had been interrupted repeatedly that afternoon by a "succession of glitches" in the communication system. In fact Grissom had been grumbling about the problems and had hung a Texas-sized lemon on the spacecraft which he had brought from his own tree in Texas.[2]

This tragedy demanded a thorough investigation into the cause of the accident. The only conclusion at which they could arrive was that the fire had started in or near a bunch of wires in front of Grissom's couch. A spark from the wire ignited flammable materials nearby that burned explosively in the pure oxygen atmosphere in the cockpit of Apollo I.

A three thousand page report of the investigation was highly critical of NASA and the builders of the spacecraft. Wiring was rerouted and covered with better insulation. Combustibles on spacecraft were replaced with flame-proof materials. The atmosphere in the cockpit was changed to a less volatile mixture of 60 percent oxygen and 40 percent nitrogen until after lift-off when it would slowly convert to pure oxygen. To make escape easier in emergencies, a hatch was devised that could be unlatched by an astronaut in three seconds. The timetable of Apollo systems was overhauled and every component put through a succession of grueling tests that would ultimately enable the United States to put a man on the moon.

```
GBE036A
PP GBEN GSTS
DE GSRM 079A
30/1742Z OCT 67

VZCZC
VZCZC
PP GBEN
DE NASAHQ 494 303
ZNR UUUUU
P 301742Z OCT 67
FM NASA HEADQUARTERS WASHINGTON DC
TO L F GRAFFIS BENDIX FIELD ENGINEERING CORP REISTERSTOWN ROAD
    AND PAINTERS MILL LANE OWINGS MILLS MD
BT
UNCLAS
DR GEORGE MUELLER JOINS ME IN EXTENDING AN INVITATION TO YOU TO
WITNESS THE FIRST UNMANNED LAUNCH OF THE APOLLO/SATURN V. THIS
LAUNCH IS NOW SCHEDULED TUESDAY, NOVEMBER 7, 1967, 700 A.M. AT THE
JOHN F. KENNEDY SPACE CENTER, FLORIDA.
THE PRIMARY OBJECTIVE OF THE MISSION, DESIGNATED AS APOLLO 4, IS TO
TEST FOR THE FIRST TIME THE PERFORMANCE OF THE SATURN LAUNCH VEHICLE
AND APOLLO SPACECRAFT IN FULL LUNAR CONFIGURATION. THE VEHICLE WILL
BE LAUNCHED FROM COMPLEX 39 AT CAPE KENNEDY AND DIRECTED TO AN ALTI-
TUDE OF 11,400 MILES FOLLOWING A CHECK OF ALL SYSTEMS IN EARTH ORBIT.


PAGE 2 NASAHQ 494 UNCLAS
THE APOLLOOXSATURN WILL BE THE LARGEST SPACE VEHICLE EVER LAUNCHED BY
THIS COUNTRY AND REPRESENTS PERHAPS THE GREATEST SINGLE CHALLENGE WE
HAVE YET FACED IN SENDING MAN INTO SPACE.
I SINCERELY HOPE YOUR SCHEDULE WILL PERMIT YOU TO OBSERVE THE LAUNCH
AND TO SHARE IN THIS HISTORIC EVENT.
I WOULD APPRECIATE YOUR LETTING ME KNOW WHETHER OR NOT YOU WILL BE
ABLE TO ATTEND BY HAVING YOUR OFFICE CONTACT THE NASA PROTOCOL OFFICE,
CODE FGE, WASHINGT, D.C. 20546 OR BY CALLING AREA CODE 202,
963-4882.
THERE ARE A NUMBER OF GOOD MOTELS AVAILABLE AT COCOA BEACH BUT THESE
FACILITIES ARE LIMITED DURING A LAUNCH AND IT WOULD BE A GOOD IDEA
TO MAKE YOUR RESERVATIONS AS SOON AS POSSIBLE IF YOU PLAN TO ATTEND.
YOU WILL ALSO BE INTERESTED TO KNOW THAT A PROTOCOL OFFICE WILL BE
ESTABLISHED AT THE CAPE COLONY INN AT COCOA BEACH WHICH WILL PROVIDE
INFORMATION AND OTHER ASSISTANCE INCLUDING BADGES AND A DETAILED
INFORMATION PACKAGE THE DAY BEFORE THE LAUNCH.
AS YOU ARE WELL AWARE, POSTPONMENTS AND DELAYS ARE ALWAYS POSSIBLE.
SHOULD THE LAUNCH BE DELAYED OR POSTPONED, THIS INVITATION IS, OF
COURSE, EXTENDED TO COVER THE LATER DATE.
JAMES E WEBB ADMIN NASA HQS WASHDC
RT
```

On 11 October 1968, almost twenty-one months after the fatal fire, the nation watched the launching of Apollo VII. This eleven-day flight was the first United States manned flight to orbit the earth. Ground control called the flight 100 percent perfect.

By 21 December 1968, Apollo VIII was the first space craft using a Saturn V booster capable of breaking the grip of earth's gravity. Apollo VII made a flight around the moon and returned safely.[3]

What a thrilling Christmas Eve that was for Leister. I was visiting our daughter Beverly in California and missed it. It was one of the great thrills of Leister's life as he watched on TV and heard the voices of the astronauts speaking to the world from sixty miles above the moon's surface.

First Bill Andres read, "In the beginning God created the heaven and earth." Jim Lowell came on next with, "And God called the light day, and the darkness He called night." Frank Borman followed with, "And God called the dry land, earth; and the gathering together of the waters He called seas; and God saw that it was good."

The next morning, Christmas Day, Borman fired the service module engine to break free from lunar gravity and to start the return trip home to planet earth. As a half-million people watched on planet earth it was a healthy boost to American morale. After a safe landing a friend telegrammed Borman, "You have bailed out 1968." It really was therapy for a nation torn by dissent over the Viet Nam War. Again the space program was back on track, after two years of misgiving following the trauma of Apollo I.

```
BDX OWGS MLS

PLS   LET ME RESEND THIS TWX

BDX OWGS MLS

AEROSPACE SYS DIV  ANN ARBOR MICH   810-223-6041     12-27-68
11/30 AM

BENDIX FIELD ENGINEERING CORP
OWINGS MILLS, MARYLAND

ATTN: MR. L. F. GRAFFIS


TWX NUMBER S-3466

PLEASE ACCEPT MY MOST SINCERE COMPLIMENTS TO YOU AND YOUR
ORGANIZATION FOR THE OUTSTANDING JOB COMPLETED IN SUPPORT
OF APOLLO 8.  THE PERFORMANCE OF THOUSANDS OF OUR EMPLOYEES
LOCATED AT STATIONS AROUND THE WORLD AND DURING THE HOLIDAY
SEASON IS INDICATIVE OF MANAGEMENT PROFESSIONALISM AND A
TRULY MOTIVATED AND INFORMED TEAM.  EVERY EMPLOYEE AND HIS
FAMILY SHOULD ACCEPT THIS ACKNOWLEDGMENT OF THEIR PERSONAL
CONTRIBUTION OVER LONG AND TEDIOUS HOURS IN FULFILLING A MOST
VITAL ROLE.  THE SOLE LINK WITH THE THREE ASTRONAUTS WAS THE
CONTINUAL TRACKING NET WHICH FUNCTIONED THROUGHOUT THE
PERIOD OF THIS HISTORIC UNDERTAKING.  WHILE OUR COMPANY IS
PROUD TO HAVE FULFILLED THIS ASSIGNMENT, IT IS EQUALLY PROUD
OF OUR EMPLOYEES WHO MADE IT POSSIBLE.

J. LYNN HELMS
BENDIX CORP - AEROSPACE SYSTEMS DIVISION

BDX OWGS MLS
P
```

Leister with daughters Beverly and Elaine,
Easter Sunday 1969

Chapter Twenty-one
Upward and Onward

The year 1969 was to be a momentously moving year. Apollo missions offered new challenges and hazards, and things on the home front were in a state of flux. In March, Apollo IX made a successful ten-day flight to test the lunar module in an earth orbit. July 16 was set as the momentous day when Apollo XI was to attempt to fulfill President Kennedy's prediction that in ten years the United States would put a man on the moon.

Elaine had just graduated from high school in June 1969. As a graduation gift, we promised to take her to Florida for the launching of Apollo XI and after that to San Francisco to see her sister Beverly. Brit, Leister's secretary, had made reservations at the Cape far in advance for us. I was glad to have Elaine with me as Leister was involved in high-level meetings in advance of the blast-off time.

Late in the evening of July 15 Leister returned to our suite and was filled with praise for the faithfulness of the Lord. During the eleventh hour final consultations of supporting contractors, Leister was prompted to speak up and suggest that before they adjourned it would be appropriate, in his estimation, that the group would pause for a moment of prayer to seek the blessing of God on the next day's launch. His request was honored and after the meeting, his associate for two years in the enterprise, Wernher Von Braun, came to him and embraced him and thanked him.

On the morning of July 16, every road leading to the Space Center was blocked with cars from berm to berm. I was allowed to sit on the VIP stand with Leister. Elaine observed with other friends from Bendix parked along the highway. The sea of spectators was charged with tension during the countdown. The blast-off was awesome, as though one were permitted to be a spectator of cosmic pangs in the birth of a flaming comet. The only outlet for such exhilarative emotion was tears. People all around wept with me as we watched Apollo XI soar out of sight.

As we saw the successful launch, hopes were high that Apollo XI would fulfill the challenge of John F. Kennedy with months to spare. After the safe return from a landing on the moon, a small bouquet of flowers was placed on the grave of John F. Kennedy with a note saying, "Mr. President, the Eagle has landed."[1]

Called to Houston, Texas, for an award for BFEC's contribution to the Apollo program.

Leister, Elaine, and I had traveled to Florida to watch the launching of Apollo XI in Leister's new Bendix car. The company had just bought him a new Mercury Marquis. We spent a week traveling back to our home in Towson. We needed this time with Leister since Elaine and I were to take a trip west to see Beverly as a second graduation gift for Elaine.

I had been having heart trouble, and we decided for my benefit we should purchase a one-story home. It would also be convenient to move closer to the new Bendix plant in Columbia, Maryland, which was thirty-five miles from Towson.

Elaine and I made the trip by car. Beverly had left some of her things in Arkadelphia, Arkansas, where she had been attending Ouachita Baptist College, and if we traveled by car we would be able to pick up those things and take them to her in California.

After visiting with Beverly we traveled to Oregon to visit Leister's mother, brothers, and their families. How Mother Graffis enjoyed seeing us. Leister's father had died in 1955 at eighty years of age.

Concurrent with a move to a new family home on Grouse Road in Elkridge had been a move for Bendix to a brand new facility in Columbia, Maryland.

The decade of the seventies again saw Leister moving upward and onward. Instead of resting on his laurels in his new office in peaceful status quo, suddenly his whole world became metamorphic. Family circumstances led Brit and her husband to decide it was time for her retirement. After nineteen years as Leister's ambidextrous right hand, that was traumatic. In close sequence, Bendix Administration in Detroit promoted Leister to the position of executive assistant to the corporate vice president of Bendix Aerospace-Electronics. Leister would have been content to stay with the simpler world of BFEC, just five miles from our home on Grouse Road. This appointment made it necessary for Leister to commute thirty-five miles daily to an office on 17th and Kay Streets in the hub of the nation's capital.

In his new role he was to explore Capitol Hill with eyes and ears open for business opportunities for all of Bendix. While hobnobbing in legislative circles he would observe the demise of the reputation of a world-honored president. From his desk he had a ringside seat on Watergate, just a few blocks away. He also saw the remnants of devastation to public areas left by the waning hippie culture.

Although Leister had enjoyed his years as a world commuter, always at heart he was a hometowner. He was intrigued with Jim Rouse's vision of a dream city. The city was soon to be internationally famous as a brilliant experiment and Leister welcomed opportunities to be involved. He served on the Human Services Commission, as president of the Columbia Foundation, and on the Planning Committee for Higher Education. Howard County was sponsoring three colleges, the Dag Hammerskjold College, Antioch College, and Howard County Community College.

Always the church was his first love, and he was wholeheartedly involved as a loyal and responsible member of the Elkridge Baptist Church. He served as moderator of the church and moderator for the Howard County Baptist Association.

April 29, 1970

ALL BFEC/COMSCO EMPLOYEES:

Effective May 1, 1970, Mr. L. F. Graffis will be transferred to the Bendix-Washington office to assume responsibility for a newly-created position, reporting directly to the writer. Mr. Graffis will be personally responsible for special assignments of a high order of significance to all of Bendix. His excellent performance at Field Engineering equips him admirably for this important work.

Mr. E. Grogan Shelor, Jr. will assume the responsibilities of President of Bendix Field Engineering Corporation and Bendix Commercial Service Corporation. Mr. Shelor comes to BFEC from the Bendix Communications Division where he was Assistant General Manager. He has been employed by Bendix since 1950 with the exception of 2 1/2 years when he joined the Department of Defense. He has held Bendix engineering and management positions with many of his assignments requiring close working relationships with DoD and NASA activities of BFEC. During his tour with the DoD, Mr. Shelor was the Assistant Director of Defense Research and Engineering for Communications and Electronics. His extensive background with Field Engineering customers and markets, including NASA and DoD, will be especially beneficial to our field engineering business and to our customers.

J. Lynn Helms

Bendix

Aerospace-Electronics Company

Bendix Center
Southfield, Michigan 48075

An Operating Group of
The Bendix Corporation

June 26, 1970

ALL BFEC/COMSCO PERSONNEL:

This is to all my BFEC/COMSCO friends that gave me the thrill of
a lifetime by presenting me the finest phono-AM/FM stereo system
anyone could dream of.

For those of you not up-to-date on recent events you had a hand in,
I was called home last week by Vic Eckman (on false pretenses) to
find Messrs. Shelor, Schaeffer, Thomas and Eckman there to present
me a Heathkit AR-15 Receiver and a $100 check to purchase extras.

You can only understand in part how much this means to me, for
mere words cannot begin to express my real appreciation and thanks.
I was forced to sell my previous system when we moved to a smaller
home last fall and simply hadn't bought a new one because I couldn't
be satisfied with anything but the AR-15 and that was out of my
immediate price range. You have made one of my dreams come true.

I immediately went out and invested the $100 you gave me, plus
considerably more, in two Heathkit AS-10 Speakers, a Dual 1219
Turntable and Shure-15 Cartridge. You have never heard a finer
Stereo!

My sincerest thanks and best personal regards to all of you.

Chapter Twenty-two
Our Trust

"For thou art my hope, 0 Lord God;
Thou hast taught me from my youth;
Hitherto have I declared Thy wondrous works.
Now when I am old and grayheaded
0 God, forsake me not, until I have shown
thy strength unto this generation
and Thy power to everyone that is to come."
Selections from Psalm 71

In 1974 Leister withdrew as a member-at-large of the Boy Scouts of America. During decades of involvement as a scout leader he had tied knots, built camp fires, worked at campouts, served on district committees for Scout Camp-O-Rees and as vice president of the Baltimore Area Council. For years Bendix sponsored an annual dinner for Explorer Scouts. His dedication to scouting had earned him the Silver Beaver award.

Leister was asked to serve as trustee of the Baptist Golden Gate Seminary in San Francisco. This called for an annual trip to the west coast each April for a board meeting. This was a convenience for it gave us a routine time to visit first one then both daughters who chose California for their careers. When possible this would include a visit with Leister's family in Oregon and my family in Minnesota.

On 1 June 1973, Leister retired from Bendix. He had often said, "I could retire tomorrow and stay busy the rest of my life," and that is just what happened. In May of that year my parents had come to visit us. They were able to celebrate Leister's retirement with us and go with us to Tennessee to see Elaine graduate, *cum laude*, with a degree in Home Economics from Tennessee Tech University. Beverly came east to join us for the graduation.

Any free time since we moved to Grouse Road Leister spent building a basement study and club room. As a retirement gift from BFEC Leister had been given a fine AM/FM stereo system. When the dream rooms were finished Leister moved the stereo down so he could work in his study and listen to the music of the masters. The love for good music he developed early in life remained a lifetime avocation.

Early in June 1972 the media kept announcing hurricane warnings as Agnes moved up the coast with reports of torrential rains and hurricane winds. We felt secure since our home was on a hill. While we slept sewer water was searching for outlets at all levels. When we awoke in the morning, we found our poor cat on the basement stairs and looking further, discovered eighteen inches of water in the basement. After four days we finally were able to pump out all the water, but we found our speakers had been standing in the eighteen inches of water and were nonfunctional for weeks. Volumes of Leister's treasured records and memos were irretrievable. It was an act of God, the insurance company said, and they were not liable.

Late in the seventies Leister began to have health problems. He had been walking a daily three-and-one-half mile circuit and his health had seemed so much more vigorous than mine. My health difficulties made me happy to confine my activities to my one-floor world. In 1979 Leister had five operations. His problem started with an ulcer. He was found to have diverticulitis, and the doctors felt it necessary to remove one-third of his stomach and eighteen inches of his intestines. Recovery from this was slow, but in spite of severe pains and repeated returns to the hospital he learned to live with new limitations.

By 1984 my health continued to be a problem as I had developed diabetes in addition to my chronic heart problem. We agreed it was time to sell our home and look for a more carefree lifestyle. We began to investigate retirement homes. Friends invited us to have dinner with them at Willow Valley Inn near Lancaster, Pennsylvania.

When we saw the Willow Valley Manor we were sure we could not afford such elegance, but since we had come so far we inquired about their contracts. When we learned we could then enter for a beginning monthly fee of $850.00 for two with no advance in fees for nursing care even if one partner should continue to occupy the apartment, we were astonished. When we learned that one-third of the selling price would return to the estate at the death of both partners, it was "exceeding abundantly above all that" we had asked or thought (Eph. 3:20) We signed a contract, were accepted, and were given a moving date of June 1985.

Life in Willow Valley has far exceeded our expectations for carefree retirement. We thank the Lord daily for those who serve us and for the mercy extended to us in the gift of such a haven in which to share our golden years.

Involvement was a way of life for Leister and me. Shortly after our move to Willow Valley Manor we became involved in a ministry to homeless children who, with their mothers, found crisis shelter at the Water Street Mission in Lancaster City. As long as our health permitted we did volunteer child care there.

As we reminisce and contrast our life at Willow Valley Manor with our dust bowl beginnings, my husband and I marvel at the grace that enabled Leister to rise from a hayloft to responsible participation in many a space lift-off.

25th ANNIVERSARY OPEN HOUSE—Murray Weingarten, president of Bendix Field Engineering Corporation, cuts the anniversary cake during a celebration of the firm's 25th year of operation. Leister F. Graffis, the company's first president, now retired, looks on. The celebration on Nov. 8 included an open house of the Columbia office, a subsidiary of the Bendix Corporation. The firm works in space tracking with NASA.

Leister takes his place among the VIPs at the fortieth anniversary of BFEC. "Seest thou a man diligent in his business? He shall stand before kings; he shall not stand before mean men." (Prov. 22:29)

The governor listens as Leister speaks over a special network to BFEC employees stationed in every corner of the globe.

Reunion of old friends–Leister with Governor Donald Schaefer
and Joe Engle (center), acting president of Bendix Field Engineering

"A merry heart doeth good like a medicine." (Prov. 17:22)
Left to right–Joe Engle, president of BFEC, Honorable
Donald Schaefer, Governor of Maryland, and Leister Graffis.

Our golden years are not the end of the road, but rather a luxury lounge where we await the ultimate lift-off. We then shall take permanent residence with the One who so abundantly fulfilled the pledge we accepted as foundational in all our aspirations:

> "Delight thyself also in the Lord, and He shall give thee
> the desires of thine heart.
> Commit thy way unto the LORD; trust also in Him,
> and He shall bring it to pass." (Ps. 37:4, 5)

Our motivation in telling Leister's story is not to exalt Leister Graffis, but rather to show how, through the faithfulness of God, the weak was made strong and dimness of sight given acuity of insight. Leister and I would give one recommendation to all:

> "Oh, taste and see that the LORD is good;
> blessed is the man who trusteth in Him." (Ps. 34:8)

If
by Rudyard Kipling

> "...If you can force your heart and nerve and sinew
> To serve your turn long after they are gone'
> And so hold on when there is nothing in you
> Except the will which says to them, 'Hold on!'
>
> If you can walk with crowds and keep your virtue,
> Or walk with kings—nor lose the common touch...
>
> Yours is the Earth and everything that's in it,
> And which is more—you'll be a Man, my Son."

Leister Graffis doing volunteer babysitting at the Water Street Child Care Nursery in Lancaster, Pennsylvania.

Afterword
Leister F. Graffis "...As Ithers" Saw Him

"O wad some Pow'r the giftie gie us
To see oursels as ithers see us"
Robert Burns

"The quality that I appreciate most about Mr. Graffis is his ability to take average people and inspire them to outstanding performance, far beyond what is normally expected of them."
Mr. E. E. Evans, Vice President, Aerospace-Electronics Company

"...Mr. Graffis...demonstrated outstanding ability in his relations with his customers—they loved him."
Mr. Arthur Omberg, retired General Manager, Bendix Systems Division

"It has been my experience to observe the fifteen-year growth of the Bendix Field Engineering Company from a very small organization to an over $50 million corporate arm of Bendix Corporation. During this time Mr. Graffis was the chief executive, and his managerial capabilities are a matter of record."
Joseph Davidson, Davidson Transfer and Storage Company

"...I would judge Les Graffis as an excellent manager. Though often quiet-spoken, he is quite articulate and is not bashful about supporting his convictions. He has a strong sense of fair play, yet is a fierce competitor. I have known quite a few of his employees. I infer from that association that he was much interested in the professional growth and motivation of his employees. All whom I have known were extremely loyal to him."
J.L. Carpenter, Jr., Martin Marietta Corporation

"Mr. Graffis is a man gifted in perceiving what human nature is all about; as a result he can properly select the right man for the right slot."
Charles F. O'Donnel, M.D., plant physician

"We, in our company, have always considered his management capabilities to be exceptional. Bendix, under his management, was our most feared competitor and always came through to us as a management of high efficiency. I would personally describe Mr. Graffis as being in the elite of the techno-managers, which are a rarity today..."
Robert E. Chasen, International Telephone and Telegraph Corporation

"I considered Mr. Graffis to be a highly motivated person with a good idea of what had to be accomplished and the ability to organize available resources to achieve the results. When competing against Mr. Graffis (Bendix) I considered such contests formidable yet fair."

S. D. Heller, President, RCA Service Company

"All of us in the management of our company have come to know Les Graffis fairly well... He has everyone's respect and affection. He has been a very effective man and one who works extremely well with people. He is bright, imaginative, extremely fair in his dealings, and has an unusual understanding of the forces at work in our society today."

James W. Rouse, President, The Rouse Company

"Just prior to my contact with Mr. Graffis, as his secretary March 1951, Mr. Graffis had been given the task of planning and organizing the Field Engineering Department. This department was started with eight engineers and through the years grew to five thousand employees and two worldwide subsidiaries. During this interim, because of big contracts, it became evident that the work had to be reorganized, from whence came another major department, also another division unto itself. His contribution materially affected the capacity of the organization in the performance of very profitable results. Mr. Graffis is an effective executive and a most important contribution to management. His leadership is borne out by the enthusiasm, initiative, and loyalty of his subordinates. The employees under Mr. Graffis have been commended time and time again for their espirit de corps. He develops and trains himself as he proceeds along his career to raise his sights and encourage those under him to do so as well. He is very dedicated and loyal to the nth degree.... I was delighted to be his secretary for nineteen years."

Britannia Riggs (Mrs. Laurence E. Riggs)

"Mr. Graffis has...a high standard of ethics, great personal integrity, and a compassionate understanding for weakness of others that he would not tolerate in himself. In dealing with people, and particularly his subordinates, his approach appears consistently to be, 'All people are capable of performing well in some area or in some job.'"

Thomas O'Conner, FBI

"It is difficult to supply a fully comprehensive report concerning Leister F. Graffis...because he does have an extremely broad and successful managerial experience record in the operation of a worldwide organization, supplying and maintaining personnel at government and commercial installations...in 1964 I assisted in the establishment of the 2,500 man Bendix Launch Support Division at Cape Kennedy under the general guidance of Mr. Graffis, who was president of the Bendix Field Engineering Company.

"An outstanding attribute, possessed by Mr. Graffis was his ability to inspire loyalty, enthusiasm, and high morale, not only among his direct employees, but also in members of groups associated with the field engineering work. Customers in government and non-government organizations, and all his associates in all walks of life felt that there just wasn't anyone better than Leister. He has an amazing ability to communicate with people."

Vernon D. Hauck, Director of Engineering, Lauch Support Division

"I have an exceptionally high regard for Les...his track record of building Bendix Field Engineering from nothing to an annual sales level of approximately $80 million is unparalleled....Not a charismatic man in the sense of being able to sell himself, yet Les's honesty and solid character have always been his outstanding attribute. Anyone who knows him knows his word is as good as his bond, and he always delivers exactly what he promises. People enjoy working for him, and he has a knack of somehow extracting the best efforts from all his organizations. No problem is too tough for him, and his credo seems always to have been that the difficult can be done immediately, but the impossible must take a little longer.

"Les also has a unique capability as an intermediary, particularly in complex situations wherein the participants represent several different nations, he has the knack of finding the one workable compromise among the conflicting special interests in the countries involved. Perhaps it's empathy and the ability to relate to others, but certainly his wealth of practical common sense is the key also."

James W. Dunham, Vice President, Fansteel, Inc.

Bibliography

Barrie Congregational Church, 100 Years.

Conrad, Stein R. *A Story of Homestead Act.* Chicago: Children's Press, 1978.

Encyclopedia of Illinois. Somerset Publishers, 1980.

The Fabulous Century, Vol. 1, 1990-1910. New York: Time Life Books.

Fisher, George Park. *History of the Christian Church.* Charles Scribner and Sons, 1915.

Fite, Gilbert C. *American Agriculture and Farm Policy Since 1900.* New York: University of Oklahoma, Macmillan Co.

Kelsey, Vera. *Red River Runs North.* New York: Harper and Row Publishers, 1951.

Kingsley, Beatrice Wilson and Cousins. *The Graffis Story.* Utah: November 1983.

Life in Space. Chicago: Time Life Books.

Low, Anne Marie. *Dust Bowl Diary.* Lincoln & London, NE: University of Nebraska Press.

McElvaine, Roberta S. *The Great Depression Times Book, 1929-1941.*

North Dakota, American Guide Series. Oxford University Press, 1950.

Pearson, Gilbert T. *Birds of America.* Garden City, NY: Garden City Publishers Co., Inc., 1944.

Update, Vol. 14, No. 6 (October 1990).

Wadsworth, Wallace. *Paul Bunyan and the Great Blue Ox.* Doubleday and Co.

Notes

Chapter One
1. *The Fabulous Century, Vol. 1, 1990-1910* (New York: Time Life Books), p. 31, 35.
2. *Ibid.*, p. 49.
3. *Ibid.*, p. 30-89.

Chapter Two
1. *Encyclopedia of Illinois* (Somerset Publishers, 1980), p. 31, 68, 159.
2. *Ibid.*, p. 49, 50.
3. Beatrice Wilson Kingsley and Cousins, *The Graffis Story* (Utah, November 1983), 2-1.
4. *Encyclopedia of Illinois*, 2 of 6.

Chapter Three
1. George Park Fisher, *History of the Christian Church* (Charles Scribner and Sons, 1915), p. 381.
2. Beatrice Wilson Kingsley and Cousins, *The Graffis Story* (Utah, November 1983). 5-87, 6-32.

Chapter Four
1. Wallace Wadsworth, *Paul Bunyan and the Great Blue Ox* (Doubleday and Co.), p. 95-107.
2. *North Dakota, American Guide Series* (Oxford University Press, 1950), p. 95-107.
3. Gilbert T. Pearson, *Birds of America* (Garden City, NY: Garden City Publishers Co., Inc., 1944), p. 248, 251.

Chapter Five
1. Stein R. Conrad, *The Story of Homestead Act* (Chicago: Children's Press, 1978), p. 19.
2. *Ibid.*, p. 19.
3. *Ibid.*, p. 18.
4. Vera Kingsley, *Red River Runs North* (New York: Harper and Row Publishers, 1951), p. 208.
5. *Ibid.*, p. 227.
6. *Ibid.*, p. 223.
7. Gilbert C. Fite, *American Agriculture and Farm Policy Since 1900* (New York: University of Oklahoma, Macmillan Co.), p. 9.
8. *Ibid.*

Chapter Seven
1. Roberta S. McElvaine, *The Great Depression Times Book, 1929-1941*, p. 20, 21.
2. Anne Marie Low, *Dust Bowl Diary* (Lincoln & London, NE: University of Nebraska Press), p. 36-44.

Chapter Seventeen
1. *Life in Space* (Chicago: Time Life Books), p. 121, 122, 264.
2. *Update*, Vol. 14, No. (October 1990), p. 1.

Chapter Twenty
1. *Update.*
2. *Life in Space* (Chicago: Time Life Books), p. 122, 138-141.
3. *Ibid.*, p. 9-10.

Chapter Twenty-one
1. *Life in Space* (Chicago: Time Life Books), p. 125.